MISSISSIPPI

GUN

LAWS 2013

Mississippi Gun Laws 2013

ISBN 978-0-9828099-8-3

Library of Congress Control Number : 2013911074

First Published 2013 by:

Spring Morning Publishing

Printed in the United States of America

http://www.concealedweaponcarry.com

http://www.boycottmississippi.com

Contents/Index:

Appendicies

Introduction

This book is intended to serve as a textbook for Enhanced Carry Classes or classes designed specifically for self-defense. It does not serve the needs of a person who has no experience, never shot before or scared of a handgun. People with those issues need to attend a very basic course to learn the safety issues of a gun, the nomenclature, basic grip, shooting, cleaning, etc.

By reading this book in advance of class, you will know what to expect and be much more prepared. It is not all inclusive but covers the primary information needed to supplement the classroom instruction. Other informational sources to include videos may compliment this text to give the student an overall understanding of the things necessary for self-defense using a handgun.

Chapter One
Arrival/Fact Finding

The first thing you need to do is register and pay for your class well in advance. Seats often fill up fast and sometimes classes get overbooked quickly. If you choose to wait until later, you will probably find something else you needed to do on that day or you may find something else you want to do with the money.

When you arrive at class, the main thing you need is your brain, your pen and maybe some note taking material, as well as this book. Weapons inside a classroom pose a potential threat and should not be brought in, especially loaded unless approved by the instructor in advance. You may want to bring a pillow to sit on and be prepared for an intense 8 hours of instruction.

You will be provided a stick-on name tag for your shirt and you may select anything you want to be called, not necessarily your entire name. For instance, if your name is Sylvester, you may want to just put Sly on the name tag in big, bold, black letters so as to be seen easily.

Don't destroy the nametag throughout the day because it will be used to place on your back for the range period. But don't worry about it if the glue doesn't hold, you can get another one before going to the range if the one you have is lost or no longer sticks. Your coaches/instructors will be behind you and need to know who you are from behind.

You should also receive a study sheet that appears to be a test. It is not a test, but rather a list of the topics that are most important and will be covered throughout the morning. You may be asked to spend 5 or 10 minutes looking over the document so when you hear a particular subject covered in class, it will spark a memory cell in your brain and you can fill in the blank on the appropriate line.

The instructor will introduce himself and give a short biographical background depicting his education and training, as well as his experience with the subject matter and teaching. Afterwards, you will be expected to introduce yourself. You may be asked to tell the class your name, occupation, level of experience with a HANDGUN and what type handgun you will be using that day.

It is important and may guide the instructor at a certain pace if he knows the level of expertise the class has as a whole, while at the same time it may help him identify deficiencies that may need to be addressed individually.

When describing yourself it is not uncommon to say something like, "I have been around guns all my life." That comment can be very misleading. That could mean you were raised by your grandfather who hunted for as long as you lived with him. It could also mean that your dad raised you shooting a pistol from the time you were 4 years old and you have continued to shoot until today.

You may regularly shoot a 9mm semi-automatic, but show up at class with a .22 revolver. You should whenever you can, come to class with the gun you intend to carry on your person to defend your life. However, cost of ammunition, availability of ammunition and so on, may dictate otherwise. People often prefer to bring a .22 to class to save money which might be an indication that they can't afford to shoot their .44 magnum on the range. If that is the case, you might want to get another handgun that you can afford to shoot, because shooting enough to become proficient enough to save your life will require much practice. If you can't afford to practice on the weapon you carry, you may want to consider a .22 conversion kit if your weapon is capable of it. Otherwise sell it and get one that is. You won't lose money on a name brand gun if you sell to an individual unless you paid an outrageous price for it initially.

The instructor may use your skills in making examples throughout the day so it is important to expound upon your occupation a little. Instead of saying you are a mechanic, you might want to say something like "I am an aircraft mechanic and work on the engines but leave the structural repairs to someone else."

DO's
1. Arrive on time
2. Arrive rested and ready for the day
3. Dress with loose clothing and large front pockets
4. Be prepared to stay all day (possibly overtime)
5. Have sufficient funds to order out for lunch
6. Have your permit with you if you have one
7. Have your driver's license with you
8. Have your gun and 100 rounds of ammo
9. Have hearing and eye protection
10. Bring bottled water, preferably frozen or cold

DON'T's

1. Misrepresent your level of expertise
2. Come into class with a loaded gun
3. Arrive with no gun or an unfamiliar gun
4. Arrive with a new gun you never shot before
5. Arrive expecting this to be a basic class
6. Bring a spouse you expect to "hand feed" you
7. Register without a Mississippi driver's license
8. Bring children to class
9. Arrive with alcohol on your breath
10. Expect a refund if you cannot attend

Classroom participation is expected and questions may be asked or discussions may be started by students as well as the instructor. Handouts may be given from time to time to supplement the text and classroom instruction. Videos of current events or those with instructional merit will be shown on occasion as will slide presentations using Powerpoint. Props such as plastic non-firing guns or airsoft guns may be used in the classroom but live weapons will not be.

Statistics from the FBI, Department of Justice and major police departments will play a major role in the class that will drive the way we train.

Chapter Two

Beyond the Basics

Anybody can be taught the basics of how to shoot a handgun. When to shoot and how to defend your actions is a whole different story. People new to the idea can easily be impressed by fancy shooters, fancy guns or war stories. You could also be lulled into the long standing rules of shooting a gun for target practice or hunting which have little to nothing to do with what you need to know to defend your life. That's what this book is about, defending your life. Hopefully that is why you intend to carry a gun, not to impress your girlfriend, boyfriend or any other person. There is a huge responsibility that comes with carrying a gun and it should not be taken lightly.

Defending your life begins with situational awareness. You must me aware of your surroundings. A good video to watch that allows you test your ability to rapidly recognize and respond to a threat accurately is:

http://www.youtube.com/watch?v=ptPNdFsAUFg

The first thing you will need to be able to do is RECOGNIZE a threat and it must be done quickly. The second thing you must do is REACT to the threat in a fraction of a second and lastly, you must be able to put a ROUND on target before your adversary does. You could consider those things the 3 R's you didn't learn in school. You might notice that each of those factors include some measure of speed. I might also add that speed comes with practice…a lot of practice.

If you play golf a couple of times a year, you probably aren't very good at it. In fact, you probably are so slow there are people behind you trying to rush you through the course. The same is true with shooting a gun but the difference is, defending your life with that gun is no game. When you lose, you don't get with your buddies and lie about your handicap or that great shot you made. Losing means closing the book on your life with the final chapter stopping abruptly.

Most of us, even with the right to openly carry a gun now, will choose not to. Most people feel, even with a course of instruction that they can reasonably use their gun to protect their lives against someone who would choose to use a gun on them. Most people, when asked what it would take to push them over the edge to draw and use their firearm to take the life of another person, usually say the opponent must be threatening them with a gun, knife, etc., or harming their family.

While those responses are common and make sense, when you really peel that banana, they don't make enough sense for you to defend your life. Let's think about this for a second. If you concluded like most people that you will carry your gun concealed, it is not going to be readily accessible in most cases. You are going to have to dig for it. Maybe you have it in the flat of your back and you are being carjacked at a red light. Maybe it's in an ankle holster and the guy with the gun on you is not going to let you bend down. Maybe it's up under your jacket, down inside your pants and you had too much for supper. Hopefully with this in mind, you can see that concealing your weapon limits your response time.

Studies have shown that the average person, not under the influence of drugs, alcohol or fatigue, has a reaction time of about seventy-five hundredths of a second. That means from the time your eyes see an object, and transmit that signal back to your brain, then your brain processes it and recognizes it as a threat, then spits out a decision to draw and sends that decision to your hand, at least three quarters of a second have passed. That doesn't count the time it will take you to find your weapon, draw it, push it forward and pull the trigger. Seconds may have passed, but if somebody already has a weapon on you, then you are probably too late. You will never make it to the third R by placing a round on target before your adversary does.

If you were to carry openly, you could cut down on that response time but even then there is no guarantee you will be able to respond quickly. If you are tired, you add to the problem. If you are not constantly aware of your surroundings, you add to the problem.

Here's our problem. Our grandfathers fought wars where there was a line of demarcation or "front line" as it was called. They were on one side and the enemy was on the other. The enemy dressed funny and talked funny, used weird looking guns and equipment. They were very distinguishable and usually stayed on their side. Our modern day wars are no longer like that. We fight in the urban areas, down dead-end streets, from house to house while civilians roam the streets watching our every move. They know who we are but we don't know who they are. The cloaks and other large items of clothing they wear could have an innocent person inside, or a vest bomb, an AK-47 rifle, grenades or handguns. We don't know who the enemy is, so an offensive war is hard to fight. We are in defense of our every move.

The same is true for us in the United States as we drive our cars at night on country highways around wooded areas. Our enemy is wildlife, not knowing where they or when they will jump out in front of us. At 55 miles per hour we travel 88 feet per second. If a deer, wild hog, or even an average size black bear were to jump in front of us at 80 feet, we would not be able to stop. The damage could only be the car, or our reactions may have steered us in front of oncoming traffic, maybe the side of the road into a tree, or upside down in a gulley or river. We know those threats exist and we are all aware of them to the point that we slow down around curves, up and down hills at night and keep our lights on bright, forever watchful.

What we also have to understand though is that we have another threat lurking out there. It is all around us a times and we don't even know it. Something we did may have prevented it and we will never know. That threat is the criminal threat. Because of them, we are not safe in our homes, churches, restaurants, theaters, parks or jogging trails.

It has been said that when seconds count, the police are only minutes away. That is not necessarily their fault but it is a true statement. One might also say that having a gun in your hand is better than having a police officer on the phone.

Did you know that the US Supreme Court has twice ruled in the last 35 years (1981 and 2005) that the police have no legal responsibility to protect you? They have ruled that the police have a responsibility for safety of society as a whole, at large, but not you individually. Then where does that put you?

Can you trust the police to protect you? At best there are only 2 of them for every 1,000 citizens in most places, so will they be there? If they are there will they be able to save your life? The Clarion Ledger reported on April 14, 2013 that more police officers (60 percent) were killed with their own weapon than by a criminal's weapon. Can they even defend themselves much less defend us? How much training do they get? The Board on Law Enforcement Officers and Training approved the "annual" firearms training program in a 7 stage timed event. Given the number of seconds at each stage, officers are only required to fire a total of 110 seconds, less than 2 minutes actually firing their guns each year.

Many of them work part-time jobs and don't have the time to practice or the funds to buy their own ammunition. The average police officer fires his weapon in the line of duty once in a 20 year career. What score do they have to achieve? They have to score a minimum of 75 percent. Our neighbor to the west of us, Louisiana has a standard firearms course for concealed weapon holders and they require the student to hit the target 100 percent of the time.

According to the FBI's Law Enforcement Officers Killed publication, there were 72 police officers killed in 2011. Of those killed only 17 were able to draw their weapons and return fire. Of the 55 remaining, only 10 made an attempt (though unsuccessful) to return fire. Of the 45 remaining, at least 43 made no attempt and were not able to draw quick enough to return fire. In two of the cases, the departments did not report whether or not the officer returned fire or attempted to do so. (see graphic on next page)

Can we trust their judgment if they arrive shooting when they come to our aid, or might we become a victim of their bullets? New York City cops arrived at a scene in front of the Empire State Building last year and shot 9 innocent bystanders. This year Los

Angeles Police Department fired into the car of innocent people in a botched attempt to kill one of their own cops, a large black male gone rogue. In one case they shot two women delivering papers in a truck similar to his, but a different make and model. One of the women was a 71 year old Hispanic mistaken for their bad cop. Bullet holes from seven officers riddled cars and trees in the surrounding area. In another incident, they riddled a white male surfer's truck with bullet holes causing him to receive injuries from a wreck.

18

Chapter Three
Shooting Statistics/Training

Statistics can provide valuable information that may tell us how we should train. Many shooters have had some sort of firearms training before, whether it was 4H, NRA, Law Enforcement, Military, Hunter Safety or whatever. They are familiar with terms like, sight picture, sight alignment, dominant eye, proper breathing, proper grip, trigger pull and so on. They have fired on courses that range from 25 to 50 yards designed for handguns.

For the purposes of this book and the type firearms training taught, we will do away with all those issues with the exception of proper grip and trigger pull. There are many types and styles of shooting but some are more fitting for soldiers in an offensive mode, police with the responsibility to chase down criminals, hunters, or competition shooters. Not that any of those techniques are wrong, they just don't fit our needs. Most of them are based on offensive shooting where the shooter is the aggressor. If you are carrying a gun to defend yourself, the title says it all. You are in a defensive mode waiting for something to happen that would cause you to draw your weapon and defend your life.

Little statistical data is kept on civilian shootings. Information like; how far the suspect was from the deceased, lighting conditions, total shots fired and so on are rarely extracted from a crime scene report. However, when a law enforcement officer is killed, the FBI obtains information from the agency that tells all those things and more. Some major police departments like New York and Miami do the same but the information is rare in a small department.

According to the FBI Law Enforcement Officers Killed publication there were 500 officers killed in the United States by firearms (543 total) between 2002 and 2011. Of the 500 killed by firearms, 232 were killed from 0-5 feet from the suspect. Another 92 were killed between 6-10 feet and 72 from 10-20 feet. Seventy-nine percent were killed in 20 feet or less from the suspect. Forty-six percent were 5 feet or less. For that reason, close quarter combat type shooting should be included in any training program teaching the student to fire from the hip, rather than arms fully extended in the Isosceles or Weaver stances. Remember 60 percent of all police officers killed in Mississippi have been killed with their own guns. We don't want to hand the gun to the bad guy.

The recommended training should be realistic type scenarios based on a range of 21 feet or less with most emphasis on the closer target rather than a farther distance. Targets that move are harder to hit so that should be incorporated in the training. Fifty four percent of the 543 officers killed were killed during some form of limited light or hours or darkness. For that reason, night fire shooting/training using dark goggles should be included in a realistic course of fire.

Studies have shown that in fast scenarios where a gun is drawn quickly an officer focuses on the gun itself as the threat and often shoots the gun hand rather than center mass. The same is true for the bad guys. If they focus on our gun and shoot it, or our hand holding it, we may lose use of that hand. For that reason, any good training program should also incorporate both strong and weak hand shooting.

Since many victims may find themselves lying on their back in the bed when a burglar arrives, they should be taught to shoot from the bed while lying on their backs. Many shootings begin with a verbal confrontation that escalates to a physical altercation that may result in a victim being knocked down with the suspect over him trying to kill him. For that reason, shooting while lying on your back should be a part of the training program.

Shooting while sitting or kneeling as if to be taking cover behind an object like a car fender are methods that should also be taught since we never know what position we are going to be in when we are forced to shoot.

Every good entry plan has a good exit plan. If we have to shoot someone, we must know at what point we stop shooting. Most people will jokingly say something like, "when I run out of bullets." Unfortunately, that is not a good answer. The right answer is when the threat no longer exists. We are not shooting to kill people, rather shooting to stop a threat. If the end result is death for the person we shoot, that is unavoidable.

A good training technique for use on the range to address the issue of when to stop shooting is the "double tap" method. In that technique, you fire two shots only, in rapid succession. You stop firing and observe your target while keeping your weapon drawn on him so as to evaluate whether or not he needs shooting again.

Everyone on a firing range during a training session should be loading, firing and dumping empties or magazines around the same time. There should be ample personnel available to serve as safety observers and/or line coaches. Each of them should be under direct observation and under the control of the instructor.

Speed is of the essence when firing at a bad guy to save your life. The draw must be quick and instinctive and the shot fired from a "point shoot" technique rather than aiming. However, the range training should begin with slow fire at the shooters' own pace. Depending upon how much time there is to shoot, speed may not come until later when the individual has had more time to practice. Speed will come with practice. Accuracy will come with practice using the proper techniques. However, accuracy on a firing range is totally different from accuracy in real-life shooting scenarios.

New York Police Department reported that in 2005, their officers fired their weapons at suspects 472 times, hitting the suspects only 82 times for a hit ratio of 17.4 percent and killed only 9 of them. Factors exist in real life scenarios that significantly drop scores seen on the firing ranges. The main factor is the stress caused by the fact that the bad guy is shooting back. It would be difficult for anybody to do their job with somebody shooting at them. Another is the fact that the suspect and probably the officer, are both moving. The suspect is taking cover and 77 percent of all shootings involved some degree of diminished light, not to mention possible adverse weather conditions.

In 2006 Los Angeles reported that their officers fired 283 rounds at suspects hitting the target 77 times for a hit ratio of 27 percent.

You should feel confident when you leave the range with a good score, but you shouldn't be over confident to the point that you think you will score equally as well in a real shooting situation.

Most police studies show an average of about 20 percent in real scenarios as opposed to 90 percent on the range. Baltimore County Police Department has a rigorous training program with much emphasis on firearms. They average 64 percent daylight hit ratio and slightly more than 40 at night. One could surmise from that, if you train more, you will be more likely to defend your life.

Video recordings found on YouTube can be valuable training aids to help students see how shooting can be improved, how little time you have to recognize a threat as seen in dash-cam shootings and so on.

To see fast drawing and shooting on target watch:

http://www.youtube.com/watch?v=Cym8vOgb3qU

To see fast shooting and shooting on multiple targets you should watch this video from YouTube:

http://www.youtube.com/watch?v=lLk1v5bSFPw

To see how important it is to be able to get your weapon out quickly, watch this video where the officer took almost 4 seconds to get his gun out of his holster. This video also brings to light another issue and that is multiple shots using a larger caliber weapon at close range does not always do the job. Sometimes it is due to drugs but not always.

http://www.youtube.com/watch?v=5gys1vioISs

An FBI report in PDF file format from the Ballistics Research Unit at the FBI Academy shows an 18 year old with no drugs or alcohol in his system shot 17 times with a .223 and 40 caliber who eventually died in the hospital but not before shooting one officer and firing a total of 26 rounds from a 1911 .45 caliber, reloading from a loose box of ammunition with a broken arm. The FBI states that many people can sustain multiple gunshot wounds and continue the fight but that **SHOT PLACEMENT IS THE KEY TO STOPPING A THREAT.** This young man was shot all over from his neck, down his torso, with multiple shots in the hip and buttocks and the top of his left foot was almost blown away.

http://catm.com/yabbfiles/Attachments/FBI_Defensive_Systems_Unit_Ballistic_Research_Facility_FBIAcademy.pdf

Some people are misled by terms like "knock-down power," large bore, large caliber and so on. If you were to watch this YouTube video, and didn't know any better, you might choose a .44 caliber magnum since it knocks the plate further back than all the other calibers in this metal plate demonstration starting with a .22 caliber by hicock45.

http://www.youtube.com/watch?v=4MPSDjJQIv4

However, that does not equate to "knock-down" power, especially knocking down a human being. The biggest problem with this test is the fact that humans are not made of steel.

If you want to see a test that more accurately shows the effect of a bullet on a human body, you may want to look at this video.

http://www.youtube.com/watch?v=OUx1aIb2cWs

Our bodies are not made of steel plates, rather soft tissue and water. Scientific labs have tested the effects of bullets on a body by using 20 percent gelatin in a substance now called ballistic gel. It is made up of the same gelatin bought from the grocery store and several recipes can be found on YouTube. Notice in this video that was filmed using a high speed camera but slowed down for us, how little the block moves off small square strips under it. However, notice the bullet cavity created after the bullet enters the block and mushrooms one inch inside. Massive trauma damage can be seen even after the bullet passes through the 10 inch block for another inch and a half before being drawn back in by the elasticity. The bullet cavity causes omnidirectional pressure outward resulting in trauma to the internal organs, but the bullet does not pass through what might be measured as a typical human chest at 10 inches thick. As seen in the video, the round was a 165 grain HST (hydra-shock) fired from a .40 caliber Glock model 22.

If you are concerned about collateral damage (as you should be), or your ammo going through one person and then hitting an innocent person, this is an important choice of ammo and gun/caliber. You may want to make your own gelatin blocks and test various types of ammunition until you find what best meets your particular caliber.

Since the first caliber shown in the hicock45 steel plate video was a .22, we would be remiss if we didn't discuss it. People often ask what type gun they should buy. My first comment is a gun you will carry all the time because taking Murphy's Law into consideration, the second you need it and don't have it may do you in. I often get comments back that since it is so hot in Mississippi and most people prefer to carry concealed, it would have to be a small gun, maybe even a .22 and that would only make people mad.

The truth is .22 caliber bullets kill more people than any other gun in the US. Some are from rifles and some from handguns. However, the first rule of a gunfight is to bring a gun and if it has to be a .22, then so be it. We have only had one major hit-type murder case in this state in the baby boomer generation and that was done with a .22 caliber Ruger pistol. It was Judge Vincent Sherry and his wife, City Councilwoman Margaret Sherry in Biloxi in 1987. There is a good documentary on the History Channel about it and a book called *Mississippi Mud*.

Domestic hogs are often killed in Mississippi using a single shot rifle loaded with a .22 caliber short. If the round hits them between the eyes, they drop to their knees instantly. One shot off center could lead to the need for a .45 with multiple shots to take the big animal down, just because shot placement wasn't accurate the first time.

Another issue about a .22 caliber is the fact that it is very dangerous due to the small high speed bullet taking its path of least resistance. If it hits a bone, say inside the rib cage, it could deflect to the other side, taking out vital organs with it before stopping. Don't ever underestimate the power and danger of a .22 caliber bullet. Nobody is suggesting that you should arm yourself with a .22 as a primary weapon, but it would be better than no weapon at all and a good starter weapon for ladies until they get used to the loud bang. It can also be a good back-up weapon.

My second choice in weapons is any weapon of a larger caliber that can be concealed easily so as to carry all the time, but one that can be converted to a .22. Glocks, Sigs, Berettas, Taurus, EAA, Kimbra, etc. can but I don't think Springfield or Smith and Wessons can. This is a very simple process that can be done in 30 seconds or less. Please review this video of a Sig Sauer P226 conversion:

http://www.youtube.com/watch?v=oYcSPqbzNd0

This is a very important issue because most people cannot afford to shoot large caliber weapons enough to practice proficiency due to the cost and wear and tear on their wrists. Conversion kits provide a remedy to this by offering you the same feel of the weapon, the same functionality and familiarization. If you practice with a gun other than the one you carry because your ammo costs too much or is too hard to carry, you need to get rid of that gun and get one that is convertible. If you couldn't afford the price of gas in a

Hummer, you would need to sell it and buy a car with better gas mileage. The same is true for your gun. But guns don't lose their value and the good news is, you can sell it without losing money and may even make a profit unless you paid an outrageous price for it in the first place.

Concerned about the lack of recoil with the .22? Ever shot a big shotgun or hard-kicking rifle at a can and noticed every bit of the recoil? How about when you shot a large animal with it? Do you remember the kick then? Not likely. Most police officers write in post-shooting reports that they don't remember the recoil or using the sights.

Chapter Four
Improving Your Skills

There are all sorts of things you can do to improve your skills. Practice is the most important but you don't want to practice doing the wrong thing so it is also important to understand fundamentals. The two things that will bite you with a pistol in self-defense shooting are grip and trigger pull. It has been said that trigger pull accounts for 95 percent of your accuracy. You can take all those other things you have learned about shooting that apply to offensive style shooting and throw them out the window for now. Not that there is no place for them, but there is very little need for them in self-defense shooting.

If you take that deep breath and slowly let it out after a bad guy already has the drop on you, there is only one reason to do that. It is to savor that last breath because it will likely be the last one you ever take. Nobody is going to stand there and wait on you to get your body in the mood through relaxation techniques. Remember self-defense with a gun is real world stuff, not play or for entertainment. There is a country song called, "Here in the Real World" and those words are followed by, "it's not that easy at all, when real hearts get broken its real tears that fall." Those may not be the exact lyrics, but you get my point.

Since you are shooting at real people, your target should most often be as realistic as possible. You should be shooting on silhouette targets, man sized at up to 15 feet. A good source for these with fast shipment is http://www.pistoleer.com . They have everything from basic targets, to hostage targets to zombie targets. They will even put a picture on a target for you if you have the approval of the person in the photo. It's not likely you will get that approval from your ex-spouse or mother-in-law, so get that out of your mind.

Pistoleer sells a target with 3 shapes on it. One is a circle, one is a square and the other is triangle. Each is colored a different color. Another has a small silhouette in the middle with small circles around it in different colors with numbers in them. The Personal Defense Network has a good video on YouTube that maximizes your skills training using these targets. All of their videos are worth watching. Rob Pincus is an excellent instructor. The best video for this drill can be found here:

http://www.youtube.com/watch?v=Z4ProU2aZnw

Rob Pincus teaches you to also put a number inside each of those shapes and practice at a short distance (maybe 7 feet) shooting at the target every time your buddy calls out your target. He could call out a shape, color or number so your brain has to work in this exercise too. Once you have mastered the ability to hit the target every time, you should now factor in speed. Use a shot timer (which will be discussed shortly). When you can hit the target every time at the speed you have chosen for your goal, move back to the 14 foot line and start the process all over again, first without speed, then with it. You will find your balance between speed and accuracy. You may want to leave the range for a couple of weeks, save your money and track down ammo, then come back. Don't start over at the 7 foot line without speed, but rather start over at the 14 foot line with speed where you left off. You will then see how often you will need to practice to maintain that level of precision and accuracy.

People buy bells and whistles for their gun in hopes of improving their skills. In most cases they are either gimmicks or offer little value in skill building. A shot timer might be a piece of equipment that could help you build your skills. You can buy an average one for about $150.00. However, you can download one for your I-Phone called "Shot Timer" made by a company known as "Surefire."

The Surefire shot time is free and it has a delay feature that lets you turn it on and drop it in your shirt pocket to wait for the buzzer that tells you to shoot. It also has a sensitivity feature that you can adjust depending on the loudness of your gun. You can raise that sensitivity bar to 90 or so and shoot a pellet gun in the house without pellets to save on ammo. In addition to those features, it will even send you an e-mail with a little spread sheet documenting each shot within hundredths of a second.

My favorite bell and whistle to pick on is the night sights, mostly made with Tritium so it they will glow in the dark. If you have them on your gun they probably came on it but some people spend a great deal of money to get them afterwards. If you plan to do that, you should ask yourself, "What do night sights light up?" The answer is, "only themselves." Your next question to yourself should be, "Do they illuminate the target?" The answer to that is also, "no." Then ask yourself if you are the type person that would shoot into a rustling bush, not knowing what's on the other side. Most of us would say, "no." With that in mind, you probably wouldn't shoot in the dark either. So you really only have a window of opportunity of about a half hour before sunrise and a half hour before dark that the sights would be effective.

My next pet peeve is sights of any kind. We already know that most police shootings take place within 21 feet of the suspect. When you really break it down, most take place within 5-6 feet of the suspect. There might be a reason for that. Police are taught to approach a call without bias, not showing favoritism or dislike for either person when two neighbors are screaming at each other. The policeman arrives and stands outside arms reach with his gun side turned away so if it becomes necessary, he can step back and draw his weapon.

Unfortunately the police usually respond to the scene after the fact. People kill each other over the dumbest things. Neighbors or family members usually kill each other after a verbal confrontation that escalates to a physical confrontation and maybe one gets knocked down while the other stands over him and shoots him.

When neighbors, friends, lovers, even robbers kill each other, they are usually closer than arms reach. If they reach the point of anger that they are driven to kill, they are probably right in each other's faces. For that reason, we will most likely be closer than 5-6 feet in a shootout, probably 0-3 feet.

So, why do we need sights? Watch the news and go back over some shooting you have heard about. You will find that most are within arm's reach. So again, why do we need sights on our guns if the guns are only for self-defense?

It's hard to teach an old dog new tricks. Whether you are in your twenties or sixties, you are probably already and old dog because you have always shot guns with sights. Most people shoot rifles mostly and handguns are new to them, but they try and use the same techniques. One suggestion to train yourself to shoot without sights may be to run a strip of black electrical tape from your rear sight over the front sight, pressing down hard on the top of the barrel. Doing that will force you to shoot without aiming.

Another thing about our old lessons learned, is dominant eye, something we are all familiar with. Well guess what, you can throw that one out the window too because we shoot instinctively with both eyes open. You start by not worrying about the exact location on the target but placing a round in the general area you are focusing on and with practice you will get better and more precise. If you ever watch competition shooters you will see they shoot fast, at multiple targets, so fast, there is no way they could be aiming. That is the way you will have to shoot to save your life.

So what about laser sights? They seem to be the thing to have as a bell and whistle on a gun. Navy Seals use them and used them on Osama Bin Laden so they must be good. Well Navy Seals are aggressors always in an offensive mode and they practice all the time. What average shooters do with lasers is a totally different story. Before looking closely at that though, let's go back and look at how we shoot with sights on a pistol. We focus on the front sight with the rear sight and target slightly out of focus. With lasers we focus on the point of impact displayed by the red dot. However, when we draw, most of us don't have the red dot on the X ring. It could be as far as 2 feet off, high or low and to one side. So we move it and our hands might shake slightly as we try to get the dot on the X ring. Then, finally, we pull the trigger.

Well, sports fans, if you do that, the time it takes to get that red dot precisely where you want it in a real shooting situation will get you killed. Unless you practice an awful lot and have great muscle memory a laser will probably be detrimental to you, not advantageous.

Using the point shoot instinctive draw technique you still focus on the point of impact, but the point of impact is where you want that round to go. It doesn't move. You aren't chasing that little red or green dot around. You are focused on the X ring and you don't take your concentration off of it. Your eyes are trained on that point of impact on the target and you simply bring your gun up to your line of sight. The top of the gun will appear blurred to you and should remain so. If you bring it up too high, you will know it because you will cover the point of impact with the gun. This will take some practice. You should also shoot a few rounds first using your sights, then forget them or tape them up and go back to shooting, this time not trying to be so precise but hitting in the general area you are pointing.

This is after you are comfortable with your firm grip. If you are shooting a newer semi-automatic that has the grip on the front of the trigger guard, slightly cup your weak hand around it and pull back with your weak hand as you push forward with your strong hand. It will give you much more control of the gun and drastically reduce recoil.

Okay, so what's left in the bell and whistle drawer? A tactical flashlight may be your best choice. They are bulky when fitted on the gun and holsters are not always available for them. Mounted lights may not be a good option unless you are a member of a SWAT team. However, the concept of a light at all is outstanding, even if carried in your pocket. Unlike night sights, flashlights can light up a target. They can also serve another purpose. When you really think about it they can serve as a non-lethal force weapon. They could temporarily blind a person or make that person blink or throw his hand over his eyes, which may be the only split second you will have to take cover, and/or return fire.

These lights are being made smaller and smaller. Their brightness intensity is measured in lumens and the higher the lumen, the brighter the light. Most are LED lights and some have multiple LEDs that produce on average about 180 lumens. Try to find one in the 200 plus range. They will usually run about $50 or less. Everybody needs a flashlight at one time or another.

41

If it is not a flashlight though, you had better be thinking of some means of distracting a person trying to kill you because most likely you don't even have your gun out and won't be able to quick draw on him. You may resort to some extreme as bad as pulling him toward you and kissing him in the mouth, or if you are a female you may jerk up your top and flash your breast at him. If you are standing next to a potted plant, you may throw dirt in his eyes or if you are drinking coffee, you may throw that in his eyes. You may look over his shoulder and yell, "Watch out, he's got a gun too," as if somebody else was really back there. Whatever works in the given situation but you might want to consider the ability to render a distraction as a higher priority than shooting.

Given the fact these people trying to kill you or rob you are right in your face, what about the way you hold the gun, your stance and so on? Most instructors teach two primary stances. One is Isosceles where your feet are shoulder width apart, knees slightly bent, leaning forward towards the target slightly with both arms fully extended. The other is the Weaver stance where the strong side foot is slightly back, the back more erect, the strong arm fully extended and the weak arm bent at the elbow serving as a support.

Well those are fine and look cool on cop shows. However, if you are only a few feet away and try that, the bad guy might take your gun right out of your hand or render it inoperable. All it takes is a hard forward grasp on a semi-automatic pointed at you and a quick death grip around the muzzle to render many of them useless. If the slide goes back the slightest amount, the gun will not fire. The same is true if it is a revolver pointed at you. Grabbing a gun is not a good option. However it may be the only option short of dying. You may not be successful, and the gun may go off in the struggle but it may miss a vital area and still save your life. If you can grab a revolver around the top and sides of the cylinder, the bad guy won't be able to pull the trigger (unless the hammer is back). He has one finger competing against all 5 of your fingers and the strength of your hand with a death grip around the cylinder and it won't turn. It has to turn in order to fire.

That's fine if it is the bad guy that has the gun on you, but if you have the gun on him, you don't want to be that close to him. You want to be a close as you can but whenever possible, outside arms reach or even lunging distance. You know that the stances mentioned earlier are not going to work so you had better be thinking along the lines of another approach. You may not be able to clear enough distance between you and him so you will have to draw and fire from just above the holster, at the hip or by the side of your stomach. Sometimes when people are shot, they keep coming. For that reason, you may want to shoot with your strong hand only, keeping your weak hand free to push the aggressor away from you, possibly requiring multiple shots to stop the threat. You should always fire until the threat no longer exists. That might be one round or 14 rounds, but you will have to articulate your actions to a police officer or court if charged.

Most lawyers will tell you not to say anything and that's probably good advice. However many people feel intimidated by a cop and are scared not to cooperate which may influence his decision as to whether or not to arrest you. Again though, most lawyers will probably tell you that spending one night in jail is better than spending 30 years if a statement you made comes back to haunt you later.

Shooting somebody is a very serious matter and should never be taken lightly. A gun is not for a hot head trying to settle a dispute or even a score. It's not to shake at the guy who cut you off in traffic, or sped down your street while children were present.

It is for defending your life only. If you are carrying one to impress your boyfriend, girlfriend, or for any other reason, or don't think you can control yourself with it, you should leave it at home. Don't drink alcohol or take drugs before or during the carrying of a gun. If you feel suicidal, give the gun to a trusted friend and seek help, but stay out of harm's way. Otherwise you should carry it with you all the time.

Chapter Five

Range Safety and Procedures

Ranges are configured differently and policies are often based on instructor demands or insurance policies. In any event **safety is always the most important issue on the range**. You may be asked to assist in putting up target frames and targets. For the purposes of this book the range safety and procedures will be listed below:

All weapons should be unloaded with empty magazines removed from the gun and the slide locked back or cylinder open when approaching the range. Tables will most likely be provided. The student should have at least 50 rounds in his/her right front pocket if right handed or left front pocket if left handed.

Only one magazine will be needed for the course and it will most often be in the left hand of right handed shooters unless the gun has been loaded or is being fired.

All shooters will wear eye and ear protection when shooting and serving as observers or line coaches.

Believe it or not, that is not a requirement by the National Rifle Association but rather it is recommended.

All shooters should arrive with sufficient fluids to remain hydrated, especially on hot days and wear clothing suited for the forecasted weather. Classes are rarely cancelled, even during the rain. After all, what are you going to do if a bad guy is shooting at you in the rain? He's not going to allow you to run get your umbrella or call it off until a sunny day.

Shooting takes place outside in the elements with little critters and sometimes big critters in the area. For that reason it is always a good idea to have sufficient skin protection against gnats, and mosquitos and maybe even the sun. We will deal with the bigger critters when that time comes.

In most classes larger than 6, you will be divided into two teams with the least experienced shooters on the line first. The more experienced shooters will stand within arm's reach directly behind you watching over your shoulder. They are looking for both safety violations and procedural violations. They will be given instructions beforehand as to their responsibilities and what to look for. If they pat you on the back, do not turn around. Keep the weapon pointed down range at all times and turn only your head to see what they want. Do not ignore them and continue shooting. You may have your thumb behind the slide about to take off the top of your knuckle.

Listen for all commands and do exactly as told, when told. If you have a failure with your weapon it is your responsibility to know how to clear the malfunction. If you cannot do so, remove your finger from the trigger guard, raise your non-firing hand, keep the muzzle pointed down range and your coach or the instructor will come to your aid. If you didn't get all rounds off, you may be allowed to shoot "alibi" rounds by yourself while the rest of the line waits.

You really only need to know how to load your gun safely, acquire a target, shoot at it, clear malfunctions and follow step-by-step detailed directions both before and after firing. The directions will be very specific at each volley of fire, no matter what technique or what distance.

While on the range, don't remove your gun unless told by an instructor and only if you are on the line. Never point a gun at anyone unless you intend to shoot them. Always consider a gun loaded until you have personally verified that it is not. Don't take anybody's word for that. Always keep your finger out of the trigger guard until you are ready to shoot and always keep the muzzle pointed downrange and up, level with the center mass of the target.

Never move down range during a course of fire unless authorized by the instructor. Freeze if anyone yells cease fire; it doesn't have to be the instructor. Anybody can do so.

You should bring a bag for your gun accessories to include a hand towel, gun solvent/oil and extra rounds In case you have an uncorrectable malfunction, you may want to bring an extra gun if you have one.

Following the shooting of all rounds, weapons will be holstered and the entire line including instructor will move forward and begin grading targets. You may keep you targets once your score has been recorded.

Chapter Six
Course of Fire

The Mississippi Highway Patrol has not designated a specific course of fire. They enter into a Memorandum of Understanding with each instructor that requires the instructor to teach in accordance with nationally accepted standards from organizations that teach firearms training. But they suggest that you improve upon the course whenever possible. Although the entire course is supposed to last 8 hours with at least one hour in the subject of law, there is no recommended time on the range, no recommended number of rounds to fire, no recommended target and no recommended sequence of fire. There are no suggested stages or positions to be in when you fire. All this will be dictated by instructor experience and whether or not he follows a particular organization's training rules, using their materials.

Depending on which instructor you hire, your curriculum could be quite different. You might choose a 23 year old instructor who just got his NRA Instructor certification and will likely have little experience to add value to the class. You might choose a local cop who is training part time and he may show you how to clear rooms in case you come home and see a shadow across your window. By the way, don't do that...just call 911 and let the police clear the house. You might get a competition shooter who is really good and fast at shooting, but may lack the other skills and knowledge of issues that you need to know. It's best to choose somebody that is mature and has a well-rounded background in both education and experience as well as certifications and has instructed hundreds of students.

Remember your driver's instructor in high school? Was it the little old lady that taught 4th grade math? Of course not, it was most likely a coach with a collateral duty. It was a "get-in-your-face" disciplinarian who put three kids in the back with threats of some type of discipline if they made a sound while he rode with the young driver up front. You couldn't hear a pin drop in the car. How realistic is that?

When young people new at driving go around the block and pick up their friends it will be total chaos in about 5 seconds. One kid will like heavy metal music, another rock and the other country, so there will be fighting over what to listen to on the radio. The driver will be sending and receiving text messages and/or talking on the phone.

A good instructor would put them under the same stresses on the road that they would likely face in real life. The same is true on the firing range.

The Louisiana State Police mandate a curriculum of fire. It is 12 rounds each at the 6, 10 and 15 foot line. All the shooting is standing upright, both arms out, shooting at a target with no interaction at all.

The course you are about to see is a course that will put you in almost every practical situation you could be in, when required to use your weapon. It may not be the best, but it is better than most, and there is a reason for each technique that differs with each volley of fire.

Some consideration has to take place for the level of expertise of the students. Not everybody will be an avid shooter. Not everyone will be free from physical limitations. Not everyone will be as familiar with their gun as they should be. Some people, especially women get very nervous around so many men, listening to military or law enforcement style commands barked out at them as they try to hear through Mickey Mouse ears with the sound of loud guns blasting all around them.

Some people may be elderly, with shaky hands or arms that have lost muscle mass over the years making it difficult to hold the gun up for long periods of time. All of this should be taken into consideration with flexibility to bend rather than break.

Failing a person should be the absolute last option and only when they choose to quit. Giving more than one opportunity to qualify is a must for those who are willing to do so. Sometimes minor injuries of the hand, too much stress or embarrassment on the range or whatever, may mean they have tried all they can, or all they can for that day. If that happens, hold their certificate in abeyance and call them to the side recommending that they go home and practice with a family member, then rescheduling a day later that they can come back and demonstrate their proficiency. Don't embarrass them or scoff at them. They have most likely done their best and may realize they came unprepared.

Everybody deserves another chance. Maybe they will hire you or somebody else to tutor them in order to work towards a better score next time. Your kindness and willingness to work with people will go a long way and they won't forget it.

For the purposes of this book, FBI and other major law enforcement agency statistics, as well as practical everyday situations will help guide us in the way we train at each of the stages of fire. Because of the distance most police officers are shot, sights are not important at all. The likelihood of being able to use sights given the time you will need to respond and the short distance you are from the target is slim to none. Aiming, dominant eye and all those related issues are unimportant. Both eyes should be open focused on the target, not the sights. This is a Point Shoot/Instinctive Shoot style that can help save your life. Even though most police officers are killed in a very short distance from the suspect, they are trained to arrive on a scene without bias, maintaining an arm's reach distance at a minimum with the weapon side turned away from the suspect. We, on the other hand will be the person facing a gunfight which likely begins from even a shorter distance with us right in somebody's face.

Stage 1: More than half of all police officers are killed in 10 feet or less of their adversary, often within 5-6 feet. For that reason we will begin our first stage of fire at 7 feet. Also we all know that a moving target is harder to hit than a stationary target, so it would be fruitless for us to stand still while someone shoots at us. For that reason, when we begin this stage of fire, the firing line will offset itself one target to the left. The person on the far left will not have a target in front of them. When the command of "Commence Fire" is given, the line will "side step" to the right however many steps it takes to get in front of their assigned target. (Sidestepping is extremely important because if the shooter turns, he will have his gun in the back of the person in front of him. The draw will take place simultaneously during the move and the shooter will fire 5 rounds on the target with the gun from the side, or hip position. The purpose of this technique is to keep the bad guy from getting the gun. Most people's arms are about 3 feet long. That includes you and the bad guy, and some guns are up to a foot long. At seven feet from the target, that means a suspect could easily grab your gun if you are extending both arms out in an Isosceles or Weaver type stance. (Isosceles is when you have both feet about shoulder width apart, knees bent, leaning slightly forward into the gun with both arms fully extended. Weaver is a modification of that stance with the strong foot back, standing more erect with the strong arm fully extended and the weak arm bent in a support mode.)

Stage 2: This stage of fire will begin at 14 feet with the line shifted to the right. Upon command of "commence fire," the line will sidestep to the left and this time will fire 5 rounds, with both arms fully extended since the distance between the target is great enough that the concern for the bad guy grabbing the gun is minimal. Also the ability to handle the gun and keep control during trigger pull is greater with both arms fully extended. It is not as awkward as shooting from the hip either.

Stage 3: Shooters will remain at the 14 foot line. This stage of fire will address two issues. One issue is that everyone needs to understand that if you have to shoot somebody, there comes a time when you have to stop shooting. For that reason, the shooter will fire two shots only (double-tap), in fast succession. The shooter will then observe the target with finger out of the trigger guard, but still covering the suspect (target) until given a second command by the instructor to "commence fire." This will be done a total of 3 times so as to fire 6 rounds at the target. However, the second issue to be addressed at this time is lighting. Statistics show that 77 percent of all shootings take place in some form of limited light. For that reason, it is important to simulate darkness. The instructor will provide wrap-around type safety glasses that have been painted with various numbers of coats of window tinting paint so as to duplicate various lighting conditions. The shooter will put the glasses on, load the weapon, fire the weapon, then when told to do so, turn around and walk seven steps back to the 21 feet line, turn back around, face the target and remove the goggles to observe their targets.

Stage 4: This stage of fire is exactly like the previous stage (double tap) with the exception that no dark goggles are used. The only difference is the shooter is 7 feet further away and shooting in daylight conditions.

Stage 5: This stage of fire involves shooting from two different positions. Part 1 will require the shooters to move back up to the 14 foot line for this stage of fire. The first stage of this fire will begin with 5 rounds using the strong hand only (fully extended.) In Part 2, the shooter will remain at this distance and load 5 additional rounds and fire them using the weak hand only. The shooter will draw with the strong hand, transfer it to the weak hand while the gun is pointed down range, and drop the strong hand, then fire all 5 shots with the weak hand, arm fully extended. The purpose of this exercise is to remind the shooter of the importance to be able to shoot with either hand in the event the strong hand becomes injured.

Stage 6: This stage of fire requires 6 rounds and remains at the 14 foot line. A mat will be rolled out in front of the shooter. Upon command by the instructor of "commence fire," the right handed shooters will step forward with their weak foot, while drawing and dropping to their strong knee. When the knee hits the ground, the shooter should begin and fire all 6 shots with both arms fully extended. This step addresses two issues for the shooter. The first one is to make himself/herself a smaller target for their adversary and the other is using a position of fire behind cover such as a car fender, etc.

Stage 7: This stage of fire will require the positioning of a 5 gallon plastic bucket upside down in front of the mat previously placed for kneeling shots. The shooter will load 6 rounds from behind the mat and move forward once loaded and commanded by the instructor. The shooters will take their seats on the buckets and fire the first 3 of 6 rounds as if to be in a seated position at a restaurant, etc. firing directly at the target. Once those 3 rounds have been fired, the shooters should continue to point the weapon down range with their fingers outside the trigger guard. The instructor will then command the students to spin to the right allowing the right arm to come back so the shooter is almost shooting the pistol from a rifle position. This technique is used for withdrawing the gun into the car and shooting at a hijacker at your driver window. (Note: Left handed shooters will have to shoot the same way unless they think they can convince the carjacker to go to the passenger window.)

Stage 8: Many people overlook the need for learning to shoot while lying on their backs. There are many times when a person may need to shoot from that position. One is, if you are lying in your bed and a burglar enters your bedroom causing you to draw from the nightstand. Another might be, if you are in a confrontation with someone that escalates from verbal to physical and they knock you down. They may be hovering over you with a weapon trying to kill you. Lastly, you might be shot and although injured, lying on the ground with the need to return fire. At this stage of fire, the shooters' mats will be pulled up to only a couple of feet in front of the target. The shooter will load with 6 rounds at the back of the mat when instructed to do so and then upon the second command, move forward, standing nose, to nose with the suspect (target). Upon the command of "commence fire," the shooters will fall down on their backs, rolling slightly to their weak sides, supporting themselves on their weak side elbow, then drawing their weapon and firing all 6 shots with only the strong hand fully extended.

That concludes the 8 stages of fire for this course. The targets will then be graded and scores rendered. If you would like to compare your course with the standard Mississippi Police Officer course, they begin at 9 feet, involve no side-stepping, no hip shooting, no night goggles, no sitting and no lying. They shoot from a maximum distance of 25 yards where you shoot from a maximum distance of 21 feet, with little emphasis at that distance (only 6 of 50 shots fired from 21 feet.) Because most shooting take place in 10 feet or less, we don't see the need in training for something that rarely happens.

Chapter Seven

Mississippi Law

This entire chapter is based on the copying and interpretation of these laws by the author who is not an attorney. This in no way implies legal advice and if you are not sure of the way the law is written or what it means from a truly legal standpoint, you need to consult an attorney.

The first thing you need to know about this subject or protecting yourself with a handgun is the state's definition of concealed (or deadly) weapons. You may be carrying concealed without a permit which is permissible under certain circumstances. You may be carrying concealed with a basic permit. You may be carrying concealed with an enhanced permit or you may be carrying openly in accordance with the law. For that reason, you need to know what you are carrying. That and other laws pertinent to the subject can be found summarized here. Comments will only be made under the laws that pertain to classroom material or frequently asked questions from prior classes.

97-37-1

Deadly weapons, carrying while concealed; use or attempt to use; penalties:

Paragraph (1) of Mississippi Code, Section 97-37-1 describes deadly weapons to include things like: switchblades, metallic knuckles, sawed off shotguns, slingshots and others.

Under paragraph (2) of Section 97-37-1, if you are over the age of 18 you may carry a deadly weapon OR firearms in your home and its curtilage, place of business or ANY motor vehicle without a license.

Under paragraph (3) of 97-37-1, if you are going to a firearms related sporting event, hunting, fishing, etc., you may carry the same without a permit in accordance with paragraph (3).

However, with the exception of these locations based on the new laws effective July 1, 2013, you must carry a weapon openly in any other place not restricted unless you are in possession of a concealed permit (basic or enhanced).

97-37-2

Doesn't exist

97-37-3

Deadly Weapons; Forfeiture of weapon; return upon dismissal or acquittal; confiscated firearms may be sold at auctions; proceeds of sale used to purchase bullet proof vests for seizing law enforcement agency.

97-37-4

Doesn't Exist

97-37-5

Unlawful for convicted felon to possess any firearms, or other weapons or devices; penalties; exceptions

97-37-6

Doesn't Exist

97-37-7

Deadly Weapons; persons permitted to carry weapons; bond; permit to carry weapons; grounds for denying application for permits; required weapons training course; reciprocal agreements

97-37-8

Doesn't Exist

97-37-9

Deadly weapons; defenses against indictments for carrying deadly weapons

97-37-10

Doesn't Exist

97-37-11

Repealed:

97-37-12

Doesn't Exist

97-37-13

Deadly weapons; weapons and cartridges not to be given to minor or intoxicated person

97-37-14

Possession of handgun by minor; act of delinquency; exceptions;

97-37-15

Parent or guardian not to permit minor son to have or carry weapon; penalties

97-37-16

Doesn't Exist

97-37-17

Possession of weapons by students; aiding or encouraging

97-37-18

Doesn't Exist

97-37-19

Deadly weapons; Exhibiting in rude, angry or threatening manner.

97-37-20

Doesn't Exist

97-37-21

Explosives and Weapons of Mass Destruction; false report of placing

97-37-22

Doesn't Exist

97-37-23

Unlawful possession of explosives; duty of officers to make search and to seize explosives; exception to prohibition

97-37-24

Doesn't Exist

97-37-25

Explosives and Weapons of Mass Destruction; Unlawful Use

97-37-26

Doesn't Exist

97-37-27

Fireworks; unlawful to explode in certain places

97-37-28

Doesn't Exist

97-37-29

Shooting into dwelling house

97-37-30

Willful discharge of a firearm toward the dwelling of another causing damage to property or domesticated animals or livestock

97-37-31

Silencers on firearms; armor piercing ammunition; manufacture, sale, possession or use unlawful

97-37-33

Toy pistols; sale of pistol or cartridges prohibited; cap pistols excepted

97-37-34
Doesn't Exist

97-37-35

Stolen Firearm, possession, receipt, acquisition or disposal; offense; punishment

97-37-36

Doesn't Exist

97-37-37

Enhanced Penalty for Use of Firearm during commission of felony

Honesty in Purchasing Firearms Act.

97-37-101

Short Title

97-37-103

Definition

97-37-105

Crime of Soliciting, persuading, encouraging or enticing illegal sale of firearms or ammunition.; crime of providing false information to licensed or private seller of firearms of ammunition

45-9-101

License to carry concealed pistol or revolver

95-3-1

Nuisance

97-3-15

Justifiable Homicide

Parts of this law are written in legal lingo and must be interpreted by a lawyer. However other parts that explain the right to stand your ground with no need to retreat and the right to use deadly force when your life or the life of another human being is in imminent danger seem simple enough for the layman to understand. Also it plainly tells us that if we are sued for killing someone and it is determined that the shooting was justifiable, the plaintiff must pay your legal costs, court fees and lost work expenses. It further states that if you are charged with a crime for killing someone and you are found not guilty, that you will be immune from civil action.

Chapter Eight
Review/Testing/Evaluation

Students should be given an overview of what they will be taught during the course. Then, those things promised should be taught in sufficient detail to make the student feel comfortable with the subject matter content. After the completion of all instruction, the student should be given a review to summarize and place emphasis on the most important issues, and answering questions for the student should be given a top priority.

Testing should cover all the main points and be asked in different ways, some multiple choice, some fill in the blank, some true and false and so on. The test could consist of as many as 40 questions. The test can be open book since you are not trying to grade their short-term memory, rather their ability to find the answers.

Tests may be given orally and consideration should be given to those people with other learning or reading disabilities for this purpose. Some students may opt not to take a course knowing there might be a test.

As a minimum, these are the things a student should know and be able to articulate his/her understanding.

1. Safety Procedures
2. Weapon Nomenclature
3. Proper Grip/Trigger pull
4. Concealed Carry Law
5. Enhanced Carry Law
6. Open Carry Law
7. Restricted Locations with guns
8. Deadly Force Rules
9. Justifiable Homicide Law
10. Reciprocity
11. Signage
12. Post shooting actions
13. Three examples of Federal Facilities
14. How hunting laws may affect carrying
15. Groups offering post-shooting representation
16. Giving notice to MHP about change of address
17. Permit with other ID at all times while armed
18. Length of time a permit is good for
19. Length of time the enhanced permit is good
20. Carrying of weapons in federal facilities

21. Judges orders that conflict with statute

22. How to clear stove pipe in his/her weapon

23. Who can yell **Cease Fire** in a dangerous situation

24. Distance most shootings occur

25. When a shotgun can be considered concealed

26. What weapons are authorized with a permit

27. Attorney General Opinions on this subject

28. Carrying in states without reciprocity

29. Carrying on aircraft

30. Employee/student administrative rules versus law

31. Carrying in state parks

32. Carrying in federal parks

33. Carrying in a truck under DOT rules

34. Carrying in school zones

35. When to stop shooting after starting

36. Three R's for protecting your life

37. How to clear a jam with multiple rounds feeding

38. Safety equipment required on range (2 pieces)

39. First call to make following a shooting

40. Second call to make following a shooting

Test questions could be developed around these topics and a 70 percent score required. Critiques may be used to evaluate student learning and satisfaction or the responses may be verbal or e-mail follow-up.

The range score should also be a factor for passing a student with a minimum of 70 percent on the range using a graded target.

Appendix I
Mississippi State
Laws

TITLE 45
PUBLIC SAFETY AND GOOD ORDER

WEAPONS
RESTRICTIONS UPON LOCAL REGULATION OF FIREARMS OR AMMUNITION

§ 45-9-51. Prohibition against adoption of certain ordinances

Subject to the provisions of Section 45-9-53, no county or municipality may adopt any ordinance that restricts or requires the possession, transportation, sale, transfer or ownership of firearms or ammunition or their components.

Miss. Code Ann. § 45-9-55 (2013)

§ 45-9-55. Employer not permitted to prohibit transportation or storage of firearms on employer property; exceptions; certain immunity for employer

(1) Except as otherwise provided in subsection (2) of this section, a public or private employer may not establish, maintain, or enforce any policy or rule that has the effect of prohibiting a person from transporting or storing a firearm in a locked vehicle in any parking lot, parking garage, or other designated parking area.

(2) A private employer may prohibit an employee from transporting or storing a firearm in a vehicle in a parking lot, parking garage, or other parking area the employer provides for employees to which access is restricted or limited through the use of a gate, security station or other means of restricting or limiting general public access onto the property.

(3) This section shall not apply to vehicles owned or leased by an employer and used by the employee in the course of his business.

(4) This section does not authorize a person to transport or store a firearm on any premises where the possession of a firearm is prohibited by state or federal law.

(5) A public or private employer shall not be liable in a civil action for damages resulting from or arising out of an occurrence involving

the transportation, storage, possession or use of a firearm covered by this section.

§ 45-9-101. License to carry stun gun, concealed pistol or revolver

(1) (a) The Department of Public Safety is authorized to issue licenses to carry stun guns, concealed pistols or revolvers to persons qualified as provided in this section. Such licenses shall be valid throughout the state for a period of five (5) years from the date of issuance. Any person possessing a valid license issued pursuant to this section may carry a stun gun, concealed pistol or concealed revolver.

(b) The licensee must carry the license, together with valid identification, at all times in which the licensee is carrying a stun gun, concealed pistol or revolver and must display both the license and proper identification upon demand by a law enforcement officer. A violation of the provisions of this paragraph (b) shall constitute a noncriminal violation with a penalty of Twenty-five Dollars ($ 25.00) and shall be enforceable by summons.

(2) The Department of Public Safety shall issue a license if the applicant:

(a) Is a resident of the state and has been a resident for twelve (12) months or longer immediately preceding the filing of the application. However, this residency requirement may be waived, provided the applicant possesses a valid permit from another state, is active military personnel stationed in Mississippi, or is a retired law enforcement officer establishing residency in the state;

(b) Is twenty-one (21) years of age or older;

(c) Does not suffer from a physical infirmity which prevents the safe handling of a stun gun, pistol or revolver;

(d) Is not ineligible to possess a firearm by virtue of having been convicted of a felony in a court of this state, of any other state, or of the United States without having been pardoned for same;

(e) Does not chronically or habitually abuse controlled substances to the extent that his normal faculties are impaired. It shall be presumed that an applicant chronically and habitually uses controlled substances to the extent that his faculties are impaired if the applicant has been voluntarily or involuntarily committed to a treatment facility for the abuse of a controlled substance or been found guilty of a crime under the provisions of the Uniform Controlled Substances Law or similar laws of any other state or the United States relating to controlled substances within a three-year period immediately preceding the date on which the application is submitted;

(f) Does not chronically and habitually use alcoholic beverages to the extent that his normal faculties are impaired. It shall be presumed that an applicant chronically and habitually uses alcoholic beverages to the extent that his normal faculties are impaired if the applicant has been voluntarily or involuntarily committed as an alcoholic to a treatment facility or has been convicted of two (2) or more offenses related to the use of alcohol under the laws of this state or similar laws of any other state or the United States within the three-year period immediately preceding the date on which the application is submitted;

(g) Desires a legal means to carry a stun gun, concealed pistol or revolver to defend himself;

(h) Has not been adjudicated mentally incompetent, or has waited five (5) years from the date of his restoration to capacity by court order;

(i) Has not been voluntarily or involuntarily committed to a mental institution or mental health treatment facility unless he possesses a certificate from a psychiatrist licensed in this state that he has not suffered from disability for a period of five (5) years;

(j) Has not had adjudication of guilt withheld or imposition of sentence suspended on any felony unless three (3) years have elapsed since probation or any other conditions set by the court have been fulfilled;

(k) Is not a fugitive from justice; and

(l) Is not disqualified to possess or own a weapon based on federal law.

(3) The Department of Public Safety may deny a license if the applicant has been found guilty of one or more crimes of violence constituting a misdemeanor unless three (3) years have elapsed since probation or any other conditions set by the court have been fulfilled or expunction has occurred prior to the date on which the application is submitted, or may revoke a license if the licensee has been found guilty of one or more crimes of violence within the preceding three (3) years. The department shall, upon notification by a law enforcement agency or a court and subsequent written verification, suspend a license or the processing of an application for a license if the licensee or applicant is arrested or formally charged with a crime which would disqualify such person from having a license under this section, until final disposition of the case. The provisions of subsection (7) of this section shall apply to any

suspension or revocation of a license pursuant to the provisions of this section.

(4) The application shall be completed, under oath, on a form promulgated by the Department of Public Safety and shall include only:

(a) The name, address, place and date of birth, race, sex and occupation of the applicant;

(b) The driver's license number or social security number of applicant;

(c) Any previous address of the applicant for the two (2) years preceding the date of the application;

(d) A statement that the applicant is in compliance with criteria contained within subsections (2) and (3) of this section;

(e) A statement that the applicant has been furnished a copy of this section and is knowledgeable of its provisions;

(f) A conspicuous warning that the application is executed under oath and that a knowingly false answer to any question, or the knowing submission of any false document by the applicant, subjects the applicant to criminal prosecution; and

(g) A statement that the applicant desires a legal means to carry a stun gun, concealed pistol or revolver to defend himself.

(5) The applicant shall submit only the following to the Department of Public Safety:

(a) A completed application as described in subsection (4) of this section;

(b) A full-face photograph of the applicant taken within the preceding thirty (30) days in which the head, including hair, in a size as determined by the Department of Public Safety;

(c) A nonrefundable license fee of One Hundred Dollars ($ 100.00). Costs for processing the set of fingerprints as required in paragraph (d) of this subsection shall be borne by the applicant. Honorably retired law enforcement officers shall be exempt from the payment of the license fee;

(d) A full set of fingerprints of the applicant administered by the Department of Public Safety; and

(e) A waiver authorizing the Department of Public Safety access to any records concerning commitments of the applicant to any of the treatment facilities or institutions referred to in subsection (2) and permitting access to all the applicant's criminal records.

(6) (a) The Department of Public Safety, upon receipt of the items listed in subsection (5) of this section, shall forward the full set of fingerprints of the applicant to the appropriate agencies for state and federal processing.

(b) The Department of Public Safety shall forward a copy of the applicant's application to the sheriff of the applicant's county of residence and, if applicable, the police chief of the applicant's municipality of residence. The sheriff of the applicant's county of residence and, if applicable, the police chief of the applicant's municipality of residence may, at his discretion, participate in the process by submitting a voluntary report to the Department of

Public Safety containing any readily discoverable prior information that he feels may be pertinent to the licensing of any applicant. The reporting shall be made within thirty (30) days after the date he receives the copy of the application. Upon receipt of a response from a sheriff or police chief, such sheriff or police chief shall be reimbursed at a rate set by the department.

(c) The Department of Public Safety shall, within forty-five (45) days after the date of receipt of the items listed in subsection (5) of this section:

(i) Issue the license;

(ii) Deny the application based solely on the ground that the applicant fails to qualify under the criteria listed in subsections (2) and (3) of this section. If the Department of Public Safety denies the application, it shall notify the applicant in writing, stating the ground for denial, and the denial shall be subject to the appeal process set forth in subsection (7); or

(iii) Notify the applicant that the department is unable to make a determination regarding the issuance or denial of a license within the forty-five-day period prescribed by this subsection, and provide an estimate of the amount of time the department will need to make the determination.

(d) In the event a legible set of fingerprints, as determined by the Department of Public Safety and the Federal Bureau of Investigation, cannot be obtained after a minimum of two (2) attempts, the Department of Public Safety shall determine eligibility based upon a name check by the Mississippi Highway Safety Patrol and a Federal Bureau of Investigation name check conducted by the Mississippi Highway Safety Patrol at the request of the Department of Public Safety.

(7) (a) If the Department of Public Safety denies the issuance of a license, or suspends or revokes a license, the party aggrieved may appeal such denial, suspension or revocation to the Commissioner of Public Safety, or his authorized agent, within thirty (30) days after the aggrieved party receives written notice of such denial, suspension or revocation. The Commissioner of Public Safety, or his duly authorized agent, shall rule upon such appeal within thirty (30) days after the appeal is filed and failure to rule within this thirty-day period shall constitute sustaining such denial, suspension or revocation. Such review shall be conducted pursuant to such reasonable rules and regulations as the Commissioner of Public Safety may adopt.

 (b) If the revocation, suspension or denial of issuance is sustained by the Commissioner of Public Safety, or his duly authorized agent pursuant to paragraph (a) of this subsection, the aggrieved party may file within ten (10) days after the rendition of such decision a petition in the circuit or county court of his residence for review of such decision. A hearing for review shall be held and shall proceed before the court without a jury upon the record made at the hearing before the Commissioner of Public Safety or his duly authorized agent. No such party shall be allowed to carry a stun gun, concealed pistol or revolver pursuant to the provisions of this section while any such appeal is pending.

(8) The Department of Public Safety shall maintain an automated listing of license holders and such information shall be available online, upon request, at all times, to all law enforcement agencies through the Mississippi Crime Information Center. However, the records of the department relating to applications for licenses to carry stun guns, concealed pistols or revolvers and records relating

to license holders shall be exempt from the provisions of the Mississippi Public Records Act of 1983 for a period of forty-five (45) days from the date of the issuance of the license or the final denial of an application.

(9) Within thirty (30) days after the changing of a permanent address, or within thirty (30) days after having a license lost or destroyed, the licensee shall notify the Department of Public Safety in writing of such change or loss. Failure to notify the Department of Public Safety pursuant to the provisions of this subsection shall constitute a noncriminal violation with a penalty of Twenty-five Dollars ($ 25.00) and shall be enforceable by a summons.

(10) In the event that a stun gun, concealed pistol or revolver license is lost or destroyed, the person to whom the license was issued shall comply with the provisions of subsection (9) of this section and may obtain a duplicate, or substitute thereof, upon payment of Fifteen Dollars ($ 15.00) to the Department of Public Safety, and furnishing a notarized statement to the department that such license has been lost or destroyed.

(11) A license issued under this section shall be revoked if the licensee becomes ineligible under the criteria set forth in subsection (2) of this section.

(12) (a) No less than ninety (90) days prior to the expiration date of the license, the Department of Public Safety shall mail to each licensee a written notice of the expiration and a renewal form prescribed by the department. The licensee must renew his license on or before the expiration date by filing with the department the renewal form, a notarized affidavit stating that the licensee remains qualified pursuant to the criteria specified in subsections (2) and (3) of this section, and a full set of fingerprints administered by the

Department of Public Safety or the sheriff of the county of residence of the licensee. The first renewal may be processed by mail and the subsequent renewal must be made in person. Thereafter every other renewal may be processed by mail to assure that the applicant must appear in person every ten (10) years for the purpose of obtaining a new photograph.

(i) Except as provided in this subsection, a renewal fee of Fifty Dollars ($ 50.00) shall also be submitted along with costs for processing the fingerprints;

(ii) Honorably retired law enforcement officers shall be exempt from the renewal fee; and

(iii) The renewal fee for a Mississippi resident aged sixty-five (65) years of age or older shall be Twenty-five Dollars ($ 25.00).

(b) The Department of Public Safety shall forward the full set of fingerprints of the applicant to the appropriate agencies for state and federal processing. The license shall be renewed upon receipt of the completed renewal application and appropriate payment of fees.

(c) A licensee who fails to file a renewal application on or before its expiration date must renew his license by paying a late fee of Fifteen Dollars ($ 15.00). No license shall be renewed six (6) months or more after its expiration date, and such license shall be deemed to be permanently expired. A person whose license has been permanently expired may reapply for licensure; however, an application for licensure and fees pursuant to subsection (5) of this section must be submitted, and a background investigation shall be conducted pursuant to the provisions of this section.

(13) No license issued pursuant to this section shall authorize any

person to carry a stun gun, concealed pistol or revolver into any place of nuisance as defined in Section 95-3-1, Mississippi Code of 1972; any police, sheriff or highway patrol station; any detention facility, prison or jail; any courthouse; any courtroom, except that nothing in this section shall preclude a judge from carrying a concealed weapon or determining who will carry a concealed weapon in his courtroom; any polling place; any meeting place of the governing body of any governmental entity; any meeting of the Legislature or a committee thereof; any school, college or professional athletic event not related to firearms; any portion of an establishment, licensed to dispense alcoholic beverages for consumption on the premises, that is primarily devoted to dispensing alcoholic beverages; any portion of an establishment in which beer or light wine is consumed on the premises, that is primarily devoted to such purpose; any elementary or secondary school facility; any junior college, community college, college or university facility unless for the purpose of participating in any authorized firearms-related activity; inside the passenger terminal of any airport, except that no person shall be prohibited from carrying any legal firearm into the terminal if the firearm is encased for shipment, for purposes of checking such firearm as baggage to be lawfully transported on any aircraft; any church or other place of worship; or any place where the carrying of firearms is prohibited by federal law. In addition to the places enumerated in this subsection, the carrying of a stun gun, concealed pistol or revolver may be disallowed in any place in the discretion of the person or entity exercising control over the physical location of such place by the placing of a written notice clearly readable at a distance of not less than ten (10) feet that the "carrying of a pistol or revolver is prohibited." No license issued pursuant to this section shall authorize the participants in a parade or demonstration for which a permit is required to carry a stun gun, concealed pistol or revolver.

(14) A law enforcement officer as defined in Section 45-6-3, chiefs of police, sheriffs and persons licensed as professional bondsmen pursuant to Chapter 39, Title 83, Mississippi Code of 1972, shall be exempt from the licensing requirements of this section.

(15) Any person who knowingly submits a false answer to any question on an application for a license issued pursuant to this section, or who knowingly submits a false document when applying for a license issued pursuant to this section, shall, upon conviction, be guilty of a misdemeanor and shall be punished as provided in Section 99-19-31, Mississippi Code of 1972.

(16) All fees collected by the Department of Public Safety pursuant to this section shall be deposited into a special fund hereby created in the State Treasury and shall be used for implementation and administration of this section. After the close of each fiscal year, the balance in this fund shall be certified to the Legislature and then may be used by the Department of Public Safety as directed by the Legislature.

(17) All funds received by a sheriff or police chief pursuant to the provisions of this section shall be deposited into the general fund of the county or municipality, as appropriate, and shall be budgeted to the sheriff's office or police department as appropriate.

(18) Nothing in this section shall be construed to require or allow the registration, documentation or providing of serial numbers with regard to any stun gun or firearm. Further, nothing in this section shall be construed to allow the open and unconcealed carrying of any stun gun or a deadly weapon as described in Section 97-37-1, Mississippi Code of 1972.

(19) Any person holding a valid unrevoked and unexpired license to

carry stun guns, concealed pistols or revolvers issued in another state shall have such license recognized by this state to carry stun guns, concealed pistols or revolvers. The Department of Public Safety is authorized to enter into a reciprocal agreement with another state if that state requires a written agreement in order to recognize licenses to carry stun guns, concealed pistols or revolvers issued by this state.

(20) The provisions of this section shall be under the supervision of the Commissioner of Public Safety. The commissioner is authorized to promulgate reasonable rules and regulations to carry out the provisions of this section.

(21) For the purposes of this section, the term "stun gun" means a portable device or weapon from which an electric current, impulse, wave or beam may be directed, which current, impulse, wave or beam is designed to incapacitate temporarily, injure, momentarily stun, knock out, cause mental disorientation or paralyze.

---

§ 45-9-151. Docket of deadly weapons seized

(1) Every law enforcement agency of the state or of any political subdivision thereof shall maintain a docket which shall contain a record of all deadly weapons that are seized by employees of such law enforcement agency. Such docket shall include the name of the arresting officer, the date of the arrest, the charge upon which the seizure was based, the name of the person from whom such deadly weapon was seized, the physical description of the deadly weapon, the serial number, if any, of the deadly weapon, and the chain of custody of the deadly weapon.

(2) Every deadly weapon seized by any law enforcement officer shall be entered into the docket required to be maintained pursuant to subsection (1) of this section within ten (10) days after the occurrence of such seizure.

(3) If the court orders any seized deadly weapon to be forfeited and disposed of by sale, the proceeds of such sale shall be deposited into the general fund of the governmental entity of which such law enforcement agency is a part and shall be budgeted to such law enforcement agency. The provisions of this subsection shall not apply to deadly weapons that are subject to forfeiture pursuant to Section 41-29-153, Mississippi Code of 1972.

(4) Any law enforcement officer who knowingly fails to cause a seized deadly weapon to be entered into the docket within the time limit specified in subsection (2) of this section shall be guilty of a misdemeanor and, upon conviction thereof, may be fined not more than One Thousand Dollars ($ 1,000.00). A conviction under the provisions of this section shall not be used as the basis for removal of a person from elective office.

TITLE 97

CRIMES

CRIMES AGAINST THE PERSON

§ 97-3-79. Robbery; use of deadly weapon

Every person who shall feloniously take or attempt to take from the person or from the presence the personal property of another and against his will by violence to his person or by putting such person in fear of immediate injury to his person by the exhibition of a deadly **weapon** shall be guilty of robbery and, upon conviction, shall be imprisoned for life in the state penitentiary if the penalty is so fixed by the jury; and in cases where the jury fails to fix the penalty at imprisonment for life in the state penitentiary the court shall fix the penalty at imprisonment in the state penitentiary for any term not less than three (3) years.

TITLE 97

CRIMES

OFFENSES AFFECTING HIGHWAYS, FERRIES AND WATERWAYS

§ 97-15-13. Hunting or shooting on or across streets and highways; shooting, etc., at traffic control devices

(1) (a) The provisions of this subsection shall only be applicable during the calendar days included in the open seasons on deer and turkey.

(b) It shall be unlawful for any person to hunt, if such person is in the possession of a **firearm** that is not unloaded on any street, public road, public highway, levee, or any railroad which is maintained by any railroad corporation, city, county, levee board, state or federal entity or the right-of-way of any such street, road, highway, levee or railroad.

(c) The provisions of this subsection shall not apply to any person engaged in a lawful action to protect his property or livestock.

(2) For purposes of this section, the following terms shall have the

meanings ascribed to them herein:

(a) "Right-of-way" means that part of a street, public road, public highway, levee or railroad maintained by a city, county, levee board, state or federal entity or railroad corporation and including that portion up to the adjacent property line or fence line.

(b) "Motorized vehicle" means any vehicle powered by any type of motor, including automobiles, farm vehicles, trucks, construction vehicles and all-terrain vehicles.

(c) "**Firearm**" means any **firearm** other than a handgun.

(d) "Hunt" or "hunting" means to hunt or chase or to shoot at or kill or to pursue with the intent to take, kill or wound any wild animal or wild bird with a **firearm** as defined in this subsection.

(e) "Unloaded" means that a cartridge or shell is not positioned in the barrel or magazine of the **firearm** or in a clip, magazine or retainer attached to the **firearm;** or in the case of a caplock muzzle-loading **firearm,** "unloaded" means that the cap has been removed; or in the case of a flintlock muzzle-loading **firearm,** "unloaded" means that all powder has been removed from the flashpan.

(3) If any person hunts or discharges any **firearm** in, on or across any street, public road, public highway, levee, railroad or the right-of-way thereof, such person is guilty of a misdemeanor and, upon conviction, shall be punished by a fine not less than One Hundred Dollars ($ 100.00) nor more than Five Hundred Dollars ($ 500.00) or by imprisonment in the county jail for not less than sixty (60) days nor more than six (6) months, or by both such fine and imprisonment. This subsection shall not apply to any law enforcement officer while in the performance of his official duty or

to any person engaged in a lawful action of self-defense.

(4) If any person shall willfully shoot any **firearms** or hurl any missile at any street, highway or railroad traffic light; street, highway or railroad marker or other sign for the regulation or designation of street, highway or railroad travel such person, upon conviction, shall be fined not less than One Hundred Dollars ($ 100.00) nor more than Five Hundred Dollars ($ 500.00), or be imprisoned not longer than thirty (30) days in the county jail, or both.

(5) It shall be the duty of all sheriffs, deputy sheriffs, constables, conservation officers and peace officers of this state to enforce the provisions of this section.

(6) If any subsection, paragraph, sentence, clause, phrase or any part of this section is hereafter declared to be unconstitutional or void, or if for any reason is declared to be invalid or of no effect, the remaining subsections, paragraphs, sentences, clauses, phrases or parts thereof shall be in no manner affected thereby but shall remain in full force and effect.

TITLE 97

CRIMES

CRIMES AGAINST PUBLIC PEACE AND SAFETY

§ 97-35-35. Tramps; penalty for not leaving house, etc. on request, carrying weapons, or threatening injury

Any tramp who shall enter any dwelling house, or yard, or enclosure about a dwelling house without the permission of the owner or occupant thereof, and shall not immediately depart when requested, or shall be found carrying firearms or other dangerous **weapons,** or shall do or threaten to do any injury to any person or the real or personal property of another, shall, upon conviction, be imprisoned in the county jail not more than three months.

TITLE 97

CRIMES

WEAPONS AND EXPLOSIVES
GENERAL PROVISIONS

§ 97-37-3. Deadly weapons; forfeiture of weapon; return upon dismissal or acquittal; confiscated firearms may be sold at auction; proceeds of sale used to purchase bulletproof vests for seizing law enforcement agency

(1) Any weapon used in violation of Section 97-37-1, or used in the commission of any other crime, shall be seized by the arresting officer, may be introduced in evidence, and in the event of a conviction, shall be ordered to be forfeited, and shall be disposed of as ordered by the court having jurisdiction of such offense. In the event of dismissal or acquittal of charges, such weapon shall be returned to the accused from whom it was seized.

(2) (a) If the weapon to be forfeited is merchantable, the court may order the weapon forfeited to the seizing law enforcement agency.

(b) A weapon so forfeited to a law enforcement agency may be sold at auction as provided by Sections 19-3-85 and 21-39-21 to a federally-licensed firearms dealer, with the proceeds from such sale at auction to be used to buy bulletproof vests for the seizing law enforcement agency.

§ 97-37-5. Unlawful for convicted felon to possess any firearms, or other weapons, or devices; penalties; exceptions

(1) It shall be unlawful for any person who has been convicted of a felony under the laws of this state, any other state, or of the United States to possess any firearm or any bowie knife, dirk knife, butcher knife, switchblade knife, metallic knuckles, blackjack, or any muffler or silencer for any firearm unless such person has received a pardon for such felony, has received a relief from disability pursuant to Section 925(c) of Title 18 of the United States Code, or has received a certificate of rehabilitation pursuant to subsection (3) of this section.

(2) Any person violating this section shall be guilty of a felony and, upon conviction thereof, shall be fined not more than Five Thousand Dollars ($ 5,000.00), or committed to the custody of the State Department of Corrections for not less than one (1) year nor more than ten (10) years, or both.

(3) A person who has been convicted of a felony under the laws of this state may apply to the court in which he was convicted for a certificate of rehabilitation. The court may grant such certificate in its discretion upon a showing to the satisfaction of the court that the applicant has been rehabilitated and has led a useful, productive and

101

law-abiding life since the completion of his sentence and upon the finding of the court that he will not be likely to act in a manner dangerous to public safety.

§ 97-37-7. Deadly weapons; persons permitted to carry weapons; bond; permit to carry weapon; grounds for denying application for permit; required weapons training course; reciprocal agreements

(1) (a) It shall not be a violation of Section 97-37-1 or any other statute for pistols, firearms or other suitable and appropriate weapons to be carried by duly constituted bank guards, company guards, watchmen, railroad special agents or duly authorized representatives who are not sworn law enforcement officers, agents or employees of a patrol service, guard service, or a company engaged in the business of transporting money, securities or other valuables, while actually engaged in the performance of their duties as such, provided that such persons have made a written application and paid a nonrefundable permit fee of One Hundred Dollars ($ 100.00) to the Department of Public Safety.

(b) No permit shall be issued to any person who has ever been convicted of a felony under the laws of this or any other state or of the United States. To determine an applicant's eligibility for a permit, the person shall be fingerprinted. If no disqualifying record is identified at the state level, the fingerprints shall be forwarded by the Department of Public Safety to the Federal Bureau of Investigation for a national criminal history record check. The department shall charge a fee which includes the amounts required by the Federal Bureau of Investigation and the department for the national and state criminal history record checks and any necessary costs incurred by the department for the handling and administration of the criminal history background checks. In the event a legible set of fingerprints, as determined by the Department of Public Safety and the Federal Bureau of Investigation, cannot be obtained after a minimum of three (3) attempts, the Department of

Public Safety shall determine eligibility based upon a name check by the Mississippi Highway Safety Patrol and a Federal Bureau of Investigation name check conducted by the Mississippi Highway Safety Patrol at the request of the Department of Public Safety.

(c) A person may obtain a duplicate of a lost or destroyed permit upon payment of a Fifteen Dollar ($ 15.00) replacement fee to the Department of Public Safety, if he furnishes a notarized statement to the department that the permit has been lost or destroyed.

(d) (i) No less than ninety (90) days prior to the expiration date of a permit, the Department of Public Safety shall mail to the permit holder written notice of expiration together with the renewal form prescribed by the department. The permit holder shall renew the permit on or before the expiration date by filing with the department the renewal form, a notarized affidavit stating that the permit holder remains qualified, and the renewal fee of Fifty Dollars ($ 50.00); provided, however, that honorably retired law enforcement officers shall be exempt from payment of the renewal fee. A permit holder who fails to file a renewal application on or before its expiration date shall pay a late fee of Fifteen Dollars ($ 15.00).

(ii) Renewal of the permit shall be required every four (4) years. The permit of a qualified renewal applicant shall be renewed upon receipt of the completed renewal application and appropriate payment of fees.

(iii) A permit cannot be renewed six (6) months or more after its expiration date, and such permit shall be deemed to be permanently expired; the holder may reapply for an original permit as provided in this section.

(2) It shall not be a violation of this or any other statute for pistols, firearms or other suitable and appropriate weapons to be carried by Department of Wildlife, Fisheries and Parks law enforcement officers, railroad special agents who are sworn law enforcement officers, investigators employed by the Attorney General, criminal investigators employed by the district attorneys, all prosecutors, public defenders, investigators or probation officers employed by the Department of Corrections, employees of the State Auditor who are authorized by the State Auditor to perform investigative functions, or any deputy fire marshal or investigator employed by the State Fire Marshal, while engaged in the performance of their duties as such, or by fraud investigators with the Department of Human Services, or by judges of the Mississippi Supreme Court, Court of Appeals, circuit, chancery, county, justice and municipal courts, or by coroners. Before any person shall be authorized under this subsection to carry a weapon, he shall complete a weapons training course approved by the Board of Law Enforcement Officer Standards and Training. Before any criminal investigator employed by a district attorney shall be authorized under this section to carry a pistol, firearm or other weapon, he shall have complied with Section 45-6-11 or any training program required for employment as an agent of the Federal Bureau of Investigation. A law enforcement officer, as defined in Section 45-6-3, shall be authorized to carry weapons in courthouses in performance of his official duties. A person licensed under Section 45-9-101 to carry a concealed pistol, who has voluntarily completed an instructional course in the safe handling and use of firearms offered by an instructor certified by a nationally recognized organization that customarily offers firearms training, or by any other organization approved by the Department of Public Safety, shall also be authorized to carry weapons in courthouses except in courtrooms during a judicial proceeding, and any location listed in subsection (13) of Section 45-9-101, except any place of nuisance as defined in Section 95-3-1, any police, sheriff or

105

highway patrol station or any detention facility, prison or jail. The department shall promulgate rules and regulations allowing concealed pistol permit holders to obtain an endorsement on their permit indicating that they have completed the aforementioned course and have the authority to carry in these locations. This section shall in no way interfere with the right of a trial judge to restrict the carrying of firearms in the courtroom.

(3) It shall not be a violation of this or any other statute for pistols, firearms or other suitable and appropriate weapons, to be carried by any out-of-state, full-time commissioned law enforcement officer who holds a valid commission card from the appropriate out-of-state law enforcement agency and a photo identification. The provisions of this subsection shall only apply if the state where the out-of-state officer is employed has entered into a reciprocity agreement with the state that allows full-time commissioned law enforcement officers in Mississippi to lawfully carry or possess a weapon in such other states. The Commissioner of Public Safety is authorized to enter into reciprocal agreements with other states to carry out the provisions of this subsection.

§ 97-37-9. Deadly weapons; defenses against indictment for carrying deadly weapon

Any person indicted or charged for a violation of Section 97-37-1 may show as a defense:

(a) that he was threatened, and had good and sufficient reason to apprehend a serious attack from any enemy, and that he did so apprehend; or

(b) that he was traveling and was not a tramp, or was setting out on a journey and was not a tramp; or

(c) that he was a law enforcement or peace officer in the discharge of his duties; or

(d) that he was at the time in the discharge of his duties as a mail carrier; or

(e) that he was at the time engaged in transporting valuables for an express company or bank; or

(f) that he was a member of the Armed Forces of the United States, National Guard, State Militia, Emergency Management Corps, guard or patrolman in a state or municipal institution while in the performance of his official duties; or

(g) that he was in lawful pursuit of a felon; or

(h) that he was lawfully engaged in legitimate sports; or

(i) that at the time he was a company guard, bank guard,

107

watchman, or other person enumerated in Section 97-37-7, and was then actually engaged in the performance of his duties as such, and then held a valid permit from the sheriff, the commissioner of public safety, or a valid permit issued by the secretary of state prior to May 1, 1974, to carry the weapon; and the burden of proving either of said defenses shall be on the accused.

§ 97-37-13. Deadly weapons; weapons and cartridges not to be given to minor or intoxicated person

It shall not be lawful for any person to sell, give or lend to any minor under eighteen (18) years of age or person intoxicated, knowing him to be a minor under eighteen (18) years of age or in a state of intoxication, any deadly weapon, or other weapon the carrying of which concealed is prohibited, or pistol cartridge; and, on conviction thereof, he shall be punished by a fine not more than One Thousand Dollars ($ 1,000.00), or imprisoned in the county jail not exceeding one (1) year, or both.

§ 97-37-14. Possession of handgun by minor; act of delinquency; exceptions

(1) Except as otherwise provided in this section, it is an act of delinquency for any person who has not attained the age of eighteen (18) years knowingly to have any handgun in such person's possession.

(2) This section shall not apply to:

(a) Any person who is:

(i) In attendance at a hunter's safety course or a firearms safety course; or

(ii) Engaging in practice in the use of a firearm or target shooting at an established range authorized by the governing body of the jurisdiction in which such range is located or any other area where the discharge of a firearm is not prohibited; or

(iii) Engaging in an organized competition involving the use of a firearm, or participating in or practicing for a performance by an organized group under 501(c)(3) as determined by the federal internal revenue service which uses firearms as a part of such performance; or

(iv) Hunting or trapping pursuant to a valid license issued to such person by the Department of Wildlife, Fisheries and Parks or as otherwise allowed by law; or

(v) Traveling with any handgun in such person's possession being unloaded to or from any activity described in subparagraph (i), (ii), (iii) or (iv) of this paragraph (a) and paragraph (b).

(b) Any person under the age of eighteen (18) years who is on real property under the control of an adult and who has the permission of such adult to possess a handgun.

(3) This section shall not apply to any person who uses a handgun or other firearm to lawfully defend himself from imminent danger at his home or place of domicile and any such person shall not be held criminally liable for such use of a handgun or other firearm.

(4) For the purposes of this section, "handgun" means a pistol, revolver or other firearm of any description, loaded or unloaded, from which any shot, bullet or other missile can be discharged, the length of the barrel of which, not including any revolving, detachable or magazine breech, is less than sixteen (16) inches.

§ 97-37-15. Parent or guardian not to permit minor son to have or carry weapon; penalty

Any parent, guardian or custodian who shall knowingly suffer or permit any child under the age of eighteen (18) years to have or to own, or to carry concealed, in whole or in part, any weapon the carrying of which concealed is prohibited, shall be guilty of a misdemeanor, and, on conviction, shall be fined not more than One Thousand Dollars ($ 1,000.00), and shall be imprisoned not more than six (6) months in the county jail. The provisions of this section shall not apply to a minor who is exempt from the provisions of Section 97-37-14.

§ 97-37-17. Possession of weapons by students; aiding or encouraging

(1) The following definitions apply to this section:

(a) "Educational property" shall mean any public or private school building or bus, public or private school campus, grounds, recreational area, athletic field, or other property owned, used or operated by any local school board, school, college or university board of trustees, or directors for the administration of any public or private educational institution or during a school-related activity, and shall include the facility and property of the Oakley Youth Development Center, operated by the Department of Human Services; provided, however, that the term "educational property" shall not include any sixteenth section school land or lieu land on which is not located a school building, school campus, recreational area or athletic field.

(b) "Student" shall mean a person enrolled in a public or private school, college or university, or a person who has been suspended or expelled within the last five (5) years from a public or private school, college or university, or a person in the custody of the Oakley Youth Development Center, operated by the Department of Human Services, whether the person is an adult or a minor.

(c) "Switchblade knife" shall mean a knife containing a blade or blades which open automatically by the release of a spring or a similar contrivance.

(d) "Weapon" shall mean any device enumerated in subsection (2) or (4) of this section.

113

(2) It shall be a felony for any person to possess or carry, whether openly or concealed, any gun, rifle, pistol or other firearm of any kind, or any dynamite cartridge, bomb, grenade, mine or powerful explosive on educational property. However, this subsection does not apply to a BB gun, air rifle or air pistol. Any person violating this subsection shall be guilty of a felony and, upon conviction thereof, shall be fined not more than Five Thousand Dollars ($ 5,000.00), or committed to the custody of the State Department of Corrections for not more than three (3) years, or both.

(3) It shall be a felony for any person to cause, encourage or aid a minor who is less than eighteen (18) years old to possess or carry, whether openly or concealed, any gun, rifle, pistol or other firearm of any kind, or any dynamite cartridge, bomb, grenade, mine or powerful explosive on educational property. However, this subsection does not apply to a BB gun, air rifle or air pistol. Any person violating this subsection shall be guilty of a felony and, upon conviction thereof, shall be fined not more than Five Thousand Dollars ($ 5,000.00), or committed to the custody of the State Department of Corrections for not more than three (3) years, or both.

(4) It shall be a misdemeanor for any person to possess or carry, whether openly or concealed, any BB gun, air rifle, air pistol, bowie knife, dirk, dagger, slingshot, leaded cane, switchblade knife, blackjack, metallic knuckles, razors and razor blades (except solely for personal shaving), and any sharp-pointed or edged instrument except instructional supplies, unaltered nail files and clips and tools used solely for preparation of food, instruction and maintenance on educational property. Any person violating this subsection shall be guilty of a misdemeanor and, upon conviction thereof, shall be fined not more than One Thousand Dollars ($ 1,000.00), or be imprisoned

114

not exceeding six (6) months, or both.

(5) It shall be a misdemeanor for any person to cause, encourage or aid a minor who is less than eighteen (18) years old to possess or carry, whether openly or concealed, any BB gun, air rifle, air pistol, bowie knife, dirk, dagger, slingshot, leaded cane, switchblade, knife, blackjack, metallic knuckles, razors and razor blades (except solely for personal shaving) and any sharp-pointed or edged instrument except instructional supplies, unaltered nail files and clips and tools used solely for preparation of food, instruction and maintenance on educational property. Any person violating this subsection shall be guilty of a misdemeanor and, upon conviction thereof, shall be fined not more than One Thousand Dollars ($ 1,000.00), or be imprisoned not exceeding six (6) months, or both.

(6) It shall not be a violation of this section for any person to possess or carry, whether openly or concealed, any gun, rifle, pistol or other firearm of any kind on educational property if:

(a) The person is not a student attending school on any educational property;

(b) The firearm is within a motor vehicle; and

(c) The person does not brandish, exhibit or display the firearm in any careless, angry or threatening manner.

(7) This section shall not apply to:

(a) A weapon used solely for educational or school-sanctioned ceremonial purposes, or used in a school-approved program conducted under the supervision of an adult whose supervision has been approved by the school authority;

(b) Armed Forces personnel of the United States, officers and soldiers of the militia and National Guard, law enforcement personnel, any private police employed by an educational institution, State Militia or Emergency Management Corps and any guard or patrolman in a state or municipal institution, and any law enforcement personnel or guard at a state juvenile training school, when acting in the discharge of their official duties;

(c) Home schools as defined in the compulsory school attendance law, Section 37-13-91;

(d) Competitors while participating in organized shooting events;

(e) Any person as authorized in Section 97-37-7 while in the performance of his official duties;

(f) Any mail carrier while in the performance of his official duties; or

(g) Any weapon not prescribed by Section 97-37-1 which is in a motor vehicle under the control of a parent, guardian or custodian, as defined in Section 43-21-105, which is used to bring or pick up a student at a school building, school property or school function.

(8) All schools shall post in public view a copy of the provisions of this section.

§ 97-37-19. Deadly weapons; exhibiting in rude, angry, or threatening manner

If any person, having or carrying any dirk, dirk-knife, sword, sword-cane, or any deadly weapon, or other weapon the carrying of which concealed is prohibited, shall, in the presence of three or more persons, exhibit the same in a rude, angry, or threatening manner, not in necessary self-defense, or shall in any manner unlawfully use the same in any fight or quarrel, the person so offending, upon conviction thereof, shall be fined in a sum not exceeding five hundred dollars or be imprisoned in the county jail not exceeding three months, or both. In prosecutions under this section it shall not be necessary for the affidavit or indictment to aver, nor for the state to prove on the trial, that any gun, pistol, or other firearm was charged, loaded, or in condition to be discharged.

§ 97-37-29. Shooting into dwelling house

If any person shall willfully and unlawfully shoot or discharge any pistol, shotgun, rifle or firearm of any nature or description into any dwelling house or any other building usually occupied by persons, whether actually occupied or not, he shall be guilty of a felony whether or not anybody be injured thereby and, on conviction thereof, shall be punished by imprisonment in the state penitentiary for a term not to exceed ten (10) years, or by imprisonment in the county jail for not more than one (1) year, or by fine of not more than five thousand dollars ($ 5,000.00), or by both such imprisonment and fine, within the discretion of the court.

§ 97-37-30. Willful discharge of a firearm toward the dwelling of another causing damage to property or domesticated animal or livestock

A person who willfully discharges his firearm toward the dwelling of another, causing property damage to the dwelling or any domesticated animal or livestock, is guilty of a misdemeanor punishable by a fine of not more than One Thousand Dollars ($ 1,000.00) or imprisonment not exceeding twelve (12) months in the county jail, or both.

§ 97-37-31. Silencers on firearms; armor piercing ammunition; manufacture, sale, possession or use unlawful

It shall be unlawful for any person, persons, corporation or manufacturing establishment, not duly authorized under federal law, to make, manufacture, sell or possess any instrument or device which, if used on firearms of any kind, will arrest or muffle the report of said firearm when shot or fired or armor piercing ammunition as defined in federal law. Any person violating this section shall be guilty of a misdemeanor and, upon conviction, shall be fined not more than Five Hundred Dollars ($ 500.00), or imprisoned in the penitentiary not more than thirty (30) days, or both. All such instruments or devices shall be registered with the Department of Public Safety and any law enforcement agency in possession of such instruments or devices shall submit an annual inventory of such instruments and devices to the Department of Public Safety. The Commissioner of Public Safety shall document the information required by this section.

§ 97-37-35. Stolen firearms; possession, receipt, acquisition or disposal; offense; punishment

(1) It is unlawful for any person knowingly or intentionally to possess, receive, retain, acquire or obtain possession or dispose of a stolen firearm or attempt to possess, receive, retain, acquire or obtain possession or dispose of a stolen firearm.

(2) It is unlawful for any person knowingly or intentionally to sell, deliver or transfer a stolen firearm or attempt to sell, deliver or transfer a stolen firearm.

(3) Any person convicted of violating this section shall be guilty of a felony and shall be punished as follows:

(a) For the first conviction, punishment by commitment to the Department of Corrections for five (5) years;

(b) For the second and subsequent convictions, the offense shall be considered trafficking in stolen firearms punishable by commitment to the Department of Corrections for not less than fifteen (15) years.

(c) For a conviction where the offender possesses two (2) or more stolen firearms, the offense shall be considered trafficking in stolen firearms punishable by commitment to the Department of Corrections for not less than fifteen (15) years.

(4) Any person who commits or attempts to commit any other crime while in possession of a stolen firearm shall be guilty of a

separate felony of possession of a stolen firearm under this section and, upon conviction thereof, shall be punished by commitment to the Department of Corrections for five (5) years, such term to run consecutively and not concurrently with any other sentence of incarceration.

§ 97-37-37. Enhanced penalty for use of firearm during commission of felony

(1) Except to the extent that a greater minimum sentence is otherwise provided by any other provision of law, any person who uses or displays a firearm during the commission of any felony shall, in addition to the punishment provided for such felony, be sentenced to an additional term of imprisonment in the custody of the Department of Corrections of five (5) years, which sentence shall not be reduced or suspended.

(2) Except to the extent that a greater minimum sentence is otherwise provided by any other provision of law, any convicted felon who uses or displays a firearm during the commission of any felony shall, in addition to the punishment provided for such felony, be sentenced to an additional term of imprisonment in the custody of the Department of Corrections of ten (10) years, to run consecutively, not concurrently, which sentence shall not be reduced or suspended.

§ 97-37-101. Short title

Sections 97-37-101 through 97-37-105 shall be known and may be cited as the "Honesty in Purchasing Firearms Act."

TITLE 97

CRIMES

WEAPONS AND EXPLOSIVES HONESTY IN PURCHASING FIREARMS ACT

§ 97-37-103. Definition

(1) For purposes of Sections 97-37-101 through 97-37-105:

(a) "Licensed dealer" means a person who is licensed pursuant to 18 USCS, Section 923, to engage in the business of dealing in firearms.

(b) "Private seller" means a person who sells or offers for sale any firearm or ammunition.

(c) "Ammunition" means any cartridge, shell or projectile designed for use in a firearm.

(d) "Materially false information" means information that portrays an illegal transaction as legal or a legal transaction as illegal.

§ 97-37-105. Crime of soliciting, persuading, encouraging or enticing illegal sale of firearms or ammunition; crime of providing false information to licensed dealer or private seller of firearms or ammunition.

(1) Any person who knowingly solicits, persuades, encourages or entices a licensed dealer or private seller of firearms or ammunition to transfer a firearm or ammunition under circumstances which the person knows would violate the laws of this state or the United States is guilty of a felony.

(2) Any person who knowingly solicits, persuades, encourages or entices a licensed dealer or private seller of firearms or ammunition to transfer a firearm or ammunition under circumstances which the person knows would violate the laws of this state or the United States is guilty of a felony.

(3) Any person found guilty of violating the provisions of this section shall be punished by a fine not exceeding Five Thousand Dollars ($ 5,000.00) or imprisoned in the custody of the Department of Corrections for not more than three (3) years, or both.

(4) This section does not apply to a law enforcement officer acting in the officer's official capacity or to a person acting at the direction of a law enforcement officer.

TITLE 97

CRIMES

DUELING

§ 97-39-1. Giving, accepting, or carrying challenge; advising, attending or aiding duel; penalty

Every person who shall challenge another to fight a duel, or who shall send, deliver, or cause to be delivered, any written or verbal message purporting or intended to be such challenge, or who shall accept any such challenge or message, or who shall knowingly carry or deliver any such message or challenge, or who shall be present at the time of fighting any duel with deadly **weapons,** either as second, aid, or surgeon, or who shall advise or give assistance to such duel, shall, on conviction thereof, be fined in a sum not less than three hundred dollars nor exceeding one thousand dollars, or be imprisoned not less than six months in the county jail, or both.

§ 97-39-11. Fighting in public place with deadly weapon, or seconding such a fight; penalty

If any person shall be guilty of fighting in any city, town, village, or other public place, and shall in such fight use any rifle, shotgun, sword, sword-cane, pistol, dirk, bowie-knife, dirk-knife, or any other deadly weapon, or if any person shall be second or aid in such fight, the person so offending shall be fined not less than three hundred dollars, and shall be imprisoned not less than three months; and if any person shall be killed in such fight, the person so killing the other may be prosecuted and convicted as in other cases of murder.

Appendix II
Federal Laws

18 USC 922(q)(1)

Federal Gun-Free School Zones

(2)(A) It shall be unlawful for any individual knowingly to possess a firearm that has moved in or that otherwise affects interstate or foreign commerce at a place that the individual knows, or has reasonable cause to believe, is a school zone.

(B) Subparagraph (A) does not apply to the possession of a firearm--

(i) on private property not part of school grounds;

(ii) if the individual possessing the firearm is licensed to do so by the State in which the school zone is located or a political subdivision of the State, and the law of the State or political subdivision requires that, before an individual obtains such a license, the law enforcement authorities of the State or political subdivision verify that the individual is qualified under law to receive the license;

(iii) that is--

    (I)   not loaded; and

    (II)   in a locked container, or a locked firearms rack that is on a motor vehicle;

(iv) by an individual for use in a program approved by a school in the school zone;

(v) by an individual in accordance with a contract entered into between a school in the school zone and the individual or an employer of the individual;

(vi) by a law enforcement officer acting in his or her official capacity; or

(vii) that is unloaded and is possessed by an individual while traversing school premises for the purpose of gaining access to public or private lands open to hunting, if the entry on school premises is authorized by school authorities.

(3)(A) Except as provided in subparagraph (B), it shall be unlawful for any person, knowingly or with reckless disregard for the safety of another, to discharge or attempt to discharge a firearm that has moved in or that otherwise affects interstate or foreign commerce at a place that the person knows is a school zone.

(B) Subparagraph (A) does not apply to the discharge of a firearm--

(i) on private property not part of school grounds;

(ii) as part of a program approved by a school in the school zone, by an individual who is participating in the program;

(iii) by an individual in accordance with a contract entered into between a school in a school zone and the individual or an employer of the individual; or

(iv) by a law enforcement officer acting in his or her official capacity.

(4) Nothing in this subsection shall be construed as preempting or preventing a State or local government from enacting a statute establishing gun free school zones as provided in this subsection.

18 USC § 926A

INTERSTATE TRANSPORTATION OF FIREARMS

Notwithstanding any other provision of any law or any rule or regulation of a State or any political subdivision thereof, any person who is not otherwise prohibited by this chapter from transporting, shipping, or receiving a firearm shall be entitled to transport a firearm for any lawful purpose from any place where he may lawfully possess and carry such firearm to any other place where he may lawfully possess and carry such firearm if, during such transportation the firearm is unloaded, and neither the firearm nor any ammunition being transported is readily accessible or is directly accessible from the passenger compartment of such transporting vehicle: Provided, That in the case of a vehicle without a compartment separate from the driver's compartment the firearm or ammunition shall be contained in a locked container other than the glove compartment or console.

Appendix III

TSA

Rules and Regulations

Firearms and Ammunition

Traveling with Special Items

Travelers may only transport UNLOADED firearms in a locked, hard-sided container in or as checked baggage. All firearms, ammunition and firearm parts, including firearm frames and receivers, are prohibited in carry-on baggage.

Realistic replicas of firearms are also prohibited in carry-on bags and must be packed in checked baggage. Rifle scopes are permitted in carry-on and checked bags.

In addition to TSA security rules on transporting firearms, airlines, as well as state, local and international governments have additional rules that may vary by location. Please check with your airline and with states and cities you will be traveling into and out of to become familiar with their requirements and ensure you are compliant with their laws.

Law Enforcement Officers: There are certain limited exceptions for law enforcement officers who may fly armed by meeting the requirements of Title 49 CFR § 1544.219. Please read our policies for law enforcement officers traveling with firearms.

To avoid issues that could impact your travel and/or result in law enforcement action, here are some guidelines to assist you in packing your firearms and ammunition:

- All firearms must be declared to the airline during the ticket counter check-in process.
- The term firearm includes:
  - Any weapon (including a starter gun) which will, or is designed to, or may readily be converted to expel a projectile by the action of an explosive.
  - The frame or receiver of any such weapon.
  - Any firearm muffler or firearm silencer.

- Any destructive device.

*Please see, for instance, United States Code, Title 18, Part 1, Chapter 44 for information about firearm definitions.

- The firearm must be unloaded.
- The firearm must be in a hard-sided container that is locked. A locked container is defined as one that completely secures the firearm from being accessed. Locked cases that can be pulled open with little effort cannot be brought aboard the aircraft.
- ♣ If firearms are not properly declared or packaged, TSA will provide the checked bag to law enforcement for resolution with the airline. If the issue is resolved, law enforcement will release the bag to TSA so screening may be completed.
- TSA must resolve all alarms in checked baggage. If a locked container containing a firearm alarms, TSA will contact the airline, who will make a reasonable attempt to contact the owner and advise the passenger to go to the screening location. If contact is not made, the container will not be placed on the aircraft.
- If a locked container alarms during screening and is not marked as containing a declared firearm, TSA will cut the lock in order to resolve the alarm.

- Travelers should remain in the area designated by the aircraft operator or TSA representative to take the key back after the container is cleared for transportation.
- Travelers must securely pack any ammunition in fiber (such as cardboard), wood or metal boxes or other packaging specifically designed to carry small amounts of ammunition.
- Firearm magazines and ammunition clips must be securely boxed or included within a hard-sided case containing an unloaded firearm.
- Small arms ammunition, including ammunition not exceeding .75 caliber for a rifle or pistol and shotgun shells of any gauge, may be carried in the same hard-sided case as the firearm, as long as it follows the packing guidelines described above.
- TSA prohibits black powder or percussion caps used with black-powder.
- Rifle scopes are not prohibited in carry-on bags and do not need to be in the hard-sided, locked checked bag.

Guns and Firearms

Item	Carry-on	Checked
Small arms ammunition, including ammunition up to .75 caliber and shotgun shells of any gauge- Check with your airline or travel agent to see if ammunition is permitted in checked baggage on the airline you are flying. Small arms ammunitions for personal use must be securely packaged in fiber, wood or metal boxes or other packaging specifically designed to carry small amounts of ammunition. Ask about limitations or fees, if any, that apply.	No	Yes
BB guns	No	Yes
Compressed Air Guns, including rifles and pistols (to include paintball markers) - Carried in checked luggage without compressed air cylinder attached.	No	Yes

Firearms - firearms carried as checked baggage MUST be unloaded, packed in a locked hard-sided container, and declared to the airline at check-in.	No	Yes
Flare Guns - May be carried as checked baggage MUST be unloaded, packed in a locked hard-sided container, and declared to the airline at check-in. Read section on Camping.	No	Yes
Flares	No	No
Gun Lighters*	No	Yes
Gun Powder including black powder and percussion caps	No	No
Parts of Guns and Firearms	No	Yes
Pellet Guns	No	Yes
Realistic Replicas of Firearms	No	Yes

Starter Pistols - can only be carried as checked baggage and MUST be unloaded, packed in a locked hard-sided container, and declared to the airline at check-in.	No	Yes

NOTE: Check with your airline or travel agent to see if firearms are permitted in checked baggage on the airline you are flying. Ask about limitations or fees, if any, that apply.

*Permitted in checked baggage only if it does not contain lighter fluid.

From TSA website: Latest revision: 23 April 2013

Appendix IV
FAQ

FREQUENTLY ASKED QUESTIONS

Q. Can you take the Enhanced Course if you don't have your permit yet?

A. Yes, but you have to apply for your permit within 90 days after taking the course.

Q. How much does the sticker cost?

A. Nothing

Q. How long is the class certification good?

A. MHP says it is good for 5 years in accordance with Driver Services Policy 15.001.01

Q. What does the IC on the sticker stand for?

A. Instructor Certified

Q. Does IC mean I am certified to instruct?

A. No, It means you have been certified by an instructor to receive an enhnanced endorsement.

Q. Is the Enhanced part good in other states?

A. No

146

Q. Can my spouse take my certificated to MHP?

A. No, you have to personally appear.

Q. Can I qualify with a .22 caliber pistol?

A. Yes but you should qualify with the gun you will carry.

Q. If we only shoot 50 rounds, why do I need to bring 100 rounds?

A. You may not qualify the first time and have to shoot again.

Q. Is the written test open book?

A. Yes, we don't test your memory.

Q. Are all courses the same regardless of the instructor?

A. No, MHP has not standardized curriculum, rather they recommend we improve on nationally accepted firearms instructor program standards so the training you receive will depend on the instructor's education, experience and training.

Q. If I haven't applied for my permit yet, can I submit my enhanced training certificate with the package?

A. Yes, it would be best to do that so when you get your permit in the mail, it will already have the IC sticker on it.

Q. If I have a Louisiana driver's license but live in Natchez, can I get a Mississippi permit?

A. No, you have to get a Mississippi driver's license and establish residency for a year.

Q. If I am on active duty in the military stationed in Mississippi do I have to get a Mississippi driver's license?

A. No, the instructor will leave the number blank on your certificate and the Mississippi Highway Patrol will assign you a number.

Q. I had a Mississippi Firearms Permit but it expired about a year ago. Can I get it renewed or will I have to re-apply?

A. You will have to start all over in the application process.

Q. Can I carry any other kind of weapon with my permit?
A. Your Firearms Permit is only valid for pistols, revolvers and stun guns.

Q. How many states recognize and accept the Mississippi permit?
A. (left blank because of fluid nature)

Appendix V
Permit
Locations/Times

151

Permit Locations

Location	Date and Time
Jackson MHP Headquarters 1900 E. Woodrow Wilson Jackson, MS 39205 (601) 987-1265, (601) 987-1587, (601) 987-1599	Monday & Thursday 8:00 a.m.- 4:30 p.m. Security Guard Permit-Originals/Renewals Tuesday & Wednesday 8:00 a.m.- 4:30 p.m. 1st Time Applicants (Originals) and Renewals Friday No permits processed on Fridays.
Troop D 701 Hwy 82 West Greenwood, MS 38930 (662) 453-4515	Wednesday 8:00 a.m. to 11:30 a.m.
Troop E 22000 A Hwy 35 N Batesville, MS 38606 (662) 563-6400	Monday & Tuesday 8:00 a.m. to 11:30 a.m. 1:00 p.m. to 3:30 p.m.
Troop F 1103 Bratton Road New Albany, MS 38652 (662) 534-8619	Tuesday, Wednesday & Thursday 8:00 a.m. to 11:30 a.m. 1:00 p.m. to 3:30 p.m.
Troop G 987 Hwy 182 E. Starkville, MS 39759 (662) 323-5316	Thursday 8:00 a.m. to 3:00 p.m. *Effective July 1st, 2013 – 8:30 a.m. to 12:00 p.m.*
Troop H 910 Hwy 11/80 E Meridian, MS 39301 (601) 693-1926	Monday & Tuesday 8:00 a.m. to 11:30 a.m.
Troop J 36 J.M. Tatum Ind Dr. Hattiesburg, MS 39401 (601) 582-4744	Tuesday & Wednesday 8:00 a.m. to 11:30 a.m. 1:00 p.m. to 3:00 p.m.
Troop K 16741 Hwy 67 S Biloxi, MS 39532 (228)396-7400	Monday-Thursday 8:00 a.m. to 11:30 a.m. 1:00 p.m. to 3:00 p.m.
Troop M 160 Hwy 84 E Brookhaven, MS 39601 (601) 833-0508	Monday 8:30 a.m. to 11:30 a.m.

Appendix VI

Reciprocity

Reciprocity Map

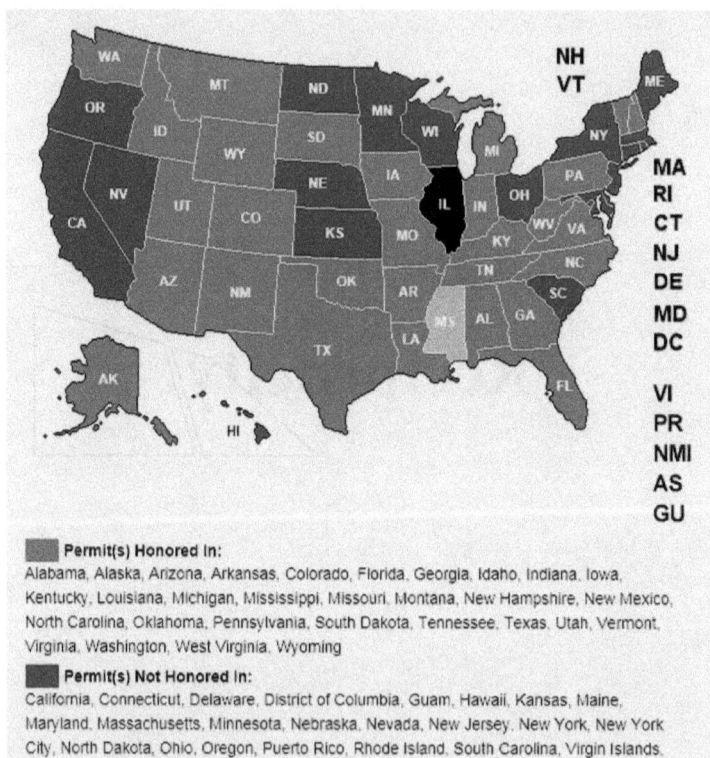

Permit(s) Honored In:
Alabama, Alaska, Arizona, Arkansas, Colorado, Florida, Georgia, Idaho, Indiana, Iowa, Kentucky, Louisiana, Michigan, Mississippi, Missouri, Montana, New Hampshire, New Mexico, North Carolina, Oklahoma, Pennsylvania, South Dakota, Tennessee, Texas, Utah, Vermont, Virginia, Washington, West Virginia, Wyoming

Permit(s) Not Honored In:
California, Connecticut, Delaware, District of Columbia, Guam, Hawaii, Kansas, Maine, Maryland, Massachusetts, Minnesota, Nebraska, Nevada, New Jersey, New York, New York City, North Dakota, Ohio, Oregon, Puerto Rico, Rhode Island, South Carolina, Virgin Islands.

Appendix VII
Judges Orders

Please go the following website to review Attorney General Opinions as they continue to come in:

http://www.concealedweaponcarry.com/apps/documents/

IN THE FIRST CIRCUIT AND CHANCERY JUDICIAL DISTRICTS OF MISSISSIPPI

IN RE: COURTHOUSE SECURITY

2012-001

AMENDED ORDER

    This matter came before the courts *sua sponte*, and after the courts having found a general need for addressing courthouse security for the protection of public employees who work at the courthouses, attorneys, parties, witnesses and the general public and, in particular, given the recent authorization for certain persons to carry weapons in courthouses and the difficulty as a result thereof in enforcing the terms of this order with respect to weapons not being allowed into courtrooms, the courts find that for the purposes of this order, the courthouse lobbies, hallways, witness rooms, and judges' chambers are effectively entrances into or part of the courtrooms and, therefore, should be deemed a part of each courtroom, and after also having found a need for addressing compliance with the rules of court during the course of court business in the courtrooms and trials, the courts further find and order as follows:

    IT IS ORDERED AND ADJUDGED that for the purposes of this order, the courthouse lobbies, hallways, witness rooms and chambers shall be and hereby are designated as entrances into and/or part of the courtrooms and, therefore, are deemed a part of each courtroom.

    IT IS FURTHER ORDERED AND ADJUDGED that weapons of any kind, including but not limited to firearms, handguns, pistols, rifles, shotguns, stun guns, knives and any other items of any kind of nature that could or may be used as a weapon shall be and hereby are prohibited from being brought into any courtroom except when in the possession of a sworn law enforcement officer.

    IT IS FURTHER ORDERED AND ADJUDGED that consistent to his statutory duties relative to courthouse security, the Sheriff of each county in this district shall be and hereby is

FILED

FEB 09 2012

MIKE
CIRCUIT CLERK

FILED: 10:18AM
February 9 20 12
DAVID "BUBBA" POUNDS, CLERK
Lori Rogers D.C.

346/321

156

required to implement electronic screening procedures as soon as practicable to enforce compliance with this order in the courtrooms of the Circuit and Chancery Courts of the First Judicial District of the State of Mississippi, but excluding the First Judicial District Adult Felony Drug Court.

IT IS FURTHER ORDERED AND ADJUDGED that backpacks, bags, briefcases, attaché cases and luggage of any kind shall be and hereby are prohibited from being brought into any courtroom thereof except when in the possession of a sworn law enforcement officer, a public employee who is working at the courthouse, attorneys and members of their staff, and members of the press.

IT IS FURTHER ORDERED AND ADJUDGED that a copy of this order shall be posted on the bulletin boards of the courthouses of the First District, distributed to the media, the Clerks of the Courts, Sheriffs and Bailiffs, and placed on the minutes of each Court.

SO ORDERED AND ADJUDGED, this the 15 day of Dec., 2011.

_____
THOMAS J. GARDNER, III, Circuit Judge

_____
JACQUELINE ESTES MASK, Chancery Judge

_____
PAUL S. FUNDERBURK, Circuit Judge

_____
TALMADGE D. LITTLEJOHN, Chancery Judge

_____
JAMES L. ROBERTS, JR., Circuit Judge

_____
MICHAEL MALSKI, Chancery Judge

_____
JIM S. POUNDS, Circuit Judge

_____
JOHN A. HATCHER, Chancery Judge

FILED

FEB 0 9 2012

M
CIRC

340/322

157

IN THE CIRCUIT COURT OF THE FIRST AND SECOND JUDICIAL DISTRICTS OF
HINDS COUNTY, MISSISSIPPI

IN RE: PUBLIC SAFETY AND WEAPON SECURITY IN THE CIRCUIT
COURTHOUSES OF HINDS COUNTY, MISSISSIPPI

ORDER PROHIBITING FIREARMS AND WEAPONS IN COURTROOMS
AND EXTENDING SAID BAN THROUGHOUT THE CIRCUIT COURTHOUSES

THIS MATTER came on *sua sponte* to be heard before the Hinds County Circuit Court regarding the public safety and security of the circuit courthouses in Hinds County. Having reviewed and considered applicable state laws, the safety and security of court personnel, active law enforcement personnel, elected officials with offices and chambers within and throughout the courthouses, and also considering the general risk of public safety for all those with business before the Court and throughout the courthouses of Hinds County; and being otherwise thoroughly advised in the premises, the undersigned finds and adjudges that Mississippi law does not prohibit or interfere with the inherent powers of the Court to restrict the carrying of firearms and other weapons, concealed or not, within the courtrooms and the adjoining offices, hallways and grounds of the courthouses encasing and in direct proximity to and leading to the courtrooms of the Court, to include but not limited to, judges' chambers, conference and jury rooms and the offices of judicial personnel, law enforcement personnel and other elected officials, in order to prevent interference with judicial proceedings and provide a safety and risk free environments in courtrooms and areas adjacent thereto.

Thus, the undersigned judge finds it reasonable, prudent and in the interest of public safety and the safe and secure operations of court proceedings, to extend the prohibition against firearms and all other weapons, concealed and unconcealed, in the courtrooms to all entrances, offices, hallways and grounds of the Hinds County Courthouses. Given the Court's close proximity to the Hinds County Sheriff's Department, the City of Jackson's Police Department and other areas where firearms and weapons are prohibited, and further considering the transportation of prisoners to and from the jails to the courthouses, and the constant volatility within and without the courtroom itself, the Court hereby restricts the carrying of any and all firearms and weapons, concealed or unconcealed, in the circuit courthouses of Hinds County Courthouse as follows:

IT IS, THEREFORE, ORDERED AND ADJUDGED that the prohibition of firearms and any other weapons, concealed or unconcealed, in the circuit court courtrooms in Hinds County Courthouses shall, and is hereby, extended to all entrances of said Hinds County circuit courthouse.

BOOK 729   PAGE 753

More to come as
time passes by.

to include all hallways, offices and grounds, during all judicial terms and in vacation, during all judicial proceedings and during the conducting of all court or courthouse business. Judicial bailiffs, all active federal, state and county law enforcement personnel and the Hinds County Sheriff, his deputies, employees and agents shall be excluded from said prohibition.

The herein public safety policy regarding firearms and other weapons is consistent with similar prohibitions in federal courtrooms and courthouses throughout the State of Mississippi (See Exhibit A).

IT IS, FURTHER, ORDERED AND ADJUDGED that all active federal, state and county law enforcement officers and others authorized by the Hinds County Sheriff shall be allowed to openly carry, or conceal, on or about his/her person any firearm or any other weapon throughout the Courthouse building, as is otherwise authorized by Mississippi law. The permission for active federal, state and county law enforcement officers to be armed within the Hinds County courthouses, *does not extend* to any Hinds County courtroom during judicial proceedings, unless authorized by the Court in writing or unless authorized by the Hinds County Sheriff, with the consent of the Court, pursuant to Mississippi law.

IT IS FURTHER ORDERED AND ADJUDGED that all persons, with or without a valid permit endorsement to carry a concealed weapon, are included within the courtroom and extended courthouse prohibitions contained in the herein order, and are hereby precluded from carrying a concealed firearm or other weapon in the circuit courthouses of Hinds County, Mississippi.

IT IS FURTHER ORDERED AND ADJUDGED that the Hinds County Sheriff shall be and is hereby responsible for monitoring and carrying out the herein order and its mandates. Further, the Hinds County Sheriff shall, in conjunction with the Court, post signage or assure that the signage at the entrances of all circuit courthouses in Hinds County, Mississippi are in compliance with the herein order; and further, that appropriate signage is in place so as to notify the public of the prohibitions included herein.

SO ORDERED AND ADJUDGED this the _29th_ day of March 2012.

STATE OF MISSISSIPPI, COUNTY OF HINDS
I, Barbara Dunn, Clerk of the Circuit Court in and for the said State and County do hereby certify that the above and foregoing is a true and correct copy of the original _____
and the same is of record in this office in _____
Book No. _____ at page _____
Given under my hand and the seal of the Circuit Court at Jackson, this the ___ day of _____ 2012.
BARBARA DUNN, Circuit Clerk
BY _____ D.C.

TOMIE T. GREEN
SENIOR CIRCUIT JUDGE

BOOK 729   PAGE   754

159

To contact Rick Ward, go to:

http://www.concealedweaponcarry.com

or

http://www.boycottmississippi.com

About the Author

Rick Ward has a B.S. in criminal justice and a Master's in education. He is a graduate of the Mississippi State Police Academy, the U.S. Army Military Police School, and the FBI National Academy.

Twice during Rick's naval career, he was stationed at the shipyard in Pascgaoula. During that time he was instrumental in teaching courses associated with firearms at three Mississippi police academies. His navy certfication and training as a Small Arms Military Instructor (SAMI) served him well when certified as an instructor by the Mississippi Board on Law Enforcement Standards and Training. During the early 1990's, he conducted judgmental shooting training at police and sheriff departments all over Mississippi, using a state of the art electronic firearms simulator. He provided executive protection and advanced firearms training in Pascagoula and police academies at Pearl, and Tupelo.

Rick was on site in New York on September 11, 2001 and responsible for navy security reactionary forces. His last assignment with the Naval Criminal Investigative Service (NCIS) led to his headquarters job in Washington, DC. He retired in February 2006.

www.ingramcontent.com/pod-product-compliance
Lightning Source LLC
Chambersburg PA
CBHW032001190326
41520CB00007B/321